SPAIN

Amadís de Gaula

TWAS 372

Amadís de Gaula

Amadís de Gaula

By FRANK PIERCE
University of Sheffield

TWAYNE PUBLISHERS

A DIVISION OF G. K. HALL & CO., BOSTON

173949

Library of Congress Cataloging in Publication Data

Pierce, Francis William, 1915–
   Amadís de Gaula.

   (Twayne's world authors series; TWAS 372: Spain)
   Bibliography: p. 167–71.
   Includes index.
   1. Amadís de Gaula.
   ISBN 0–8057–6220–5

Contents

About the Author

Frank Pierce (born in 1915) is a graduate of the Queen's University, Belfast, Northern Ireland, where he studied under the late Ignacio González-Llubera. He has also studied and resided in the United States and Spain, and has held teaching posts in the University of Liverpool and in Trinity College, Dublin. Since 1946 he has been chairman of the Department of Hispanic Studies and since 1953 professor of Spanish, and from 1964 to 1967, dean of arts, at the University of Sheffield, and he is a former president of the Association of Hispanists of Great Britain and Ireland. His publications include many studies on Spanish narrative poetry of the Golden Age, notably that of Ercilla, Balbuena, and Hojeda (his *Poesía épica del Siglo de Oro* came out in a second edition in 1968), articles on Cervantes's shorter novels and an edition of two of them, and several studies of the work of the great Portuguese poet Luís de Camões, whose epic *Os Lusíadas* he edited with introduction and notes in 1973. Frank Pierce has also taught as a visiting professor at Brown University and Case Western Reserve University and has lectured in several other American universities.

Preface

The case for writing a book in this series on the *Amadís de Gaula* (*Amadis of Gaul*) hardly needs to be made. It still stands as one of the major pieces of early literature in Spanish. Thus it belongs to the company of the *Poema del Cid* (*Poem of the Cid*), the *Libro de buen amor* (*Book of Good Love*), and the *Celestina*. Its great popularity in Spain throughout the 1500s and its immense fame and influence in Europe generally during the same period are part of literary history. Its temporary eclipse was brought about by its very appeal, which caused the appearance of many inferior successors, and, it would seem, by a genuine falling off of taste for the genre to which it belongs. This turnabout in public favor was to give Cervantes the initial idea for *Don Quixote*, although he made an honorable exception of what he called the first and the best of the novels of chivalry, namely the *Amadís*. The latter came into their own again with the revival of interest in medieval things in the age of Romanticism, and during the later 1800s. Today, as will be seen later, scholarly interest in the *Amadís* has not waned, and all serious students of Cervantes are aware of the relevance of our romance for the reading of *Don Quixote*.

On its own merits the *Amadís* has enough of the ingredients of true romance to commend itself to those attracted by enchantment, erotic adventure, and a subtle and changing plot and structure. In the case of the *Amadís* all these elements are spiced with recurring realistic treatment and even some humor. Reading tastes during our century have clearly shown a demand for several kinds of fiction, that is, in addition to the older staple of realism that has dominated the novel for so long during the past hundred years or so. Thus a love of symbolism of different kinds and a fascination for structures and forms have made Joyce, Proust, and Kafka Europe's outstanding masters of fiction during the early 1900s, while the fame of such weavers of fantasy as J. R. R. Tolkien and the growth of science fiction during later decades have clearly demonstrated that the imaginative need for romance is far from dead. There is thus no reason to regard the *Amadís* as a museum piece.

A word about the form of this monograph. Although "the *Amadís* question" accounts for a very great deal of the writing on our romance, and although this in one form or another has gone on for over half a millennium, it is now obvious that this is largely history. The *Amadís* will live as a piece of literature on its own or not at all. Therefore, the present writer makes no excuse for concentrating on its subject matter and its structures and for subordinating (in our Chapter 3) consideration of the details of its undoubtedly distinguished career. Some attention is also given in Chapter 1 to the setting in which the *Amadís* took its final form from Montalvo and to the immediately earlier period when it existed in its so-called primitive shape. Little attention is given to Montalvo's biography, chiefly because very few facts are known. In any case, a greater knowledge than we have of his life would surely throw very little light on his elaboration of material he inherited from others. The usefulness of a writer's biography for a study of his work has been greatly overemphasized, since imaginative literature is essentially autonomous. Where biographical facts are available they should be applied with great care so as to avoid distorting the true nature of a creative work and thus turning it into a veiled biography. The *Amadís* could have been completed by any man of talent who, like Montalvo, saw the significance of its tradition for the tastes and the values of the society of the Catholic Monarchs.

It will therefore be seen that this little book is mainly concerned with analyzing the contents and the form of the *Amadís*. Apart from an important study of its structure, this has not been done before in any detail. Any exploration of the riches of the *Amadís* inevitably means considerable repetition, and it is hoped that this will be understood in the attempted analysis of a complex unity.

Acknowledgments are made to the following colleagues for their kindness in supplying information and giving advice: Keith Whinnom (Exeter), R. M. Walker (Birkbeck College, London), Pamela Waley and A. D. Deyermond (Westfield College, London), R. B. Tate (Nottingham), P. E. Russell (Oxford), and Madeleine Blaess (Sheffield). Most sincere thanks are also expressed to the two departmental secretaries at Sheffield, Mrs. Audrey Stapley and Mrs. Valerie Tibenham, for their great patience and their expert preparation of the typescript of the book.

Chronology

1434   The *Paso honroso*, or "challenge of honor" by Suero de Quiñones to all comers, witnessed and written down by Pero Rodríguez de Lena (first published, 1588).

1469   Ferdinand becomes king of Aragon and marries Isabella.

1474   Isabella becomes queen of Castile and Leon, and the two kingdoms unite.

1482   Montalvo's name (as alderman, or "regidor") appears in the so-called Padrón de Alhama, a list of one hundred gentleman soldiers from Medina del Campo sent to garrison the town just taken from the Moors.

1485   *Le Morte d'Arthur*, by Sir Thomas Malory, printed by Caxton.

circa
1485   Alfonso de la Torre's famous *Visión delectable (Delightful Vision)* completed.

1490   Montalvo again listed as an alderman. The first published edition of the famous Catalan romance of chivalry *Tirant lo blanc*, by Joanot Martorell and Martí Joan de Galba.

1492   Granada taken by Ferdinand and Isabella and Moorish rule ended. First edition of Antonio de Nebrija's *Gramática sobre la lengua castellana*, and of Diego de San Pedro's *Cárcel de amor (Prison of Love)*, the most famous of the so-called sentimental novels.

1494   Title of "Catholic Monarchs" conferred upon Ferdinand and Isabella by Pope Alexander VI (a Spaniard) for their championing of the faith.

1495   *Orlando innamorato* (in its three-book form), one of the long Italian verse romances, by Matteomaria Boiardo.

circa
1495   *Grimalte y Gradissa* and *Grisel y Mirabella*, sentimental novels by Juan de Flores, completed.

1496   Probable first edition of the *Amadís de Gaula* (Seville?), according to the nineteenth-century German bibliographer F. A. Ebert, although no copy is known to have survived, and it is thus not fully authenticated.

1498   *Baladro del sabio Merlín (Cry of the Wizard Merlin)*, a Castilian version of part of the Holy Grail tales.

1499   First known edition of *Comedia de Calisto y Melibea*, universally known as *La Celestina*, by Fernando de Rojas. Also *Oliveros de Castilla y Artús de Algarbe*, a Spanish translation of a French original of 1492, and one of several pseudohistorical romances of the period.

1501   *Tristán de Leonís*, the first published Castilian version of an ancient Arthurian romance.

1504   Isabella dies, in Medina del Campo.

1505   Montalvo died before this date, when a lawsuit over the title of alderman in his family was taking place.

1508   *Amadís de Gaula* appears in Saragossa edition by Jorge de Coci Alemán, on October 30. This is the earliest authenticated edition; a unique copy survives in the British Museum.

1510   Appearance of *Sergas de Esplandián*, or Book V of the *Amadís*, by Montalvo.

CHAPTER 1

Montalvo and the Spain of His Time

THIS monograph is about one work of literature, not about all the publications of an author. Further, it is the only work to which Montalvo's name is attached (apart from its continuation), and yet, as is also well known, he is only the author in a partial sense of the romance as it is known to us through the first surviving edition, that of 1508. Again, the documented facts from Montalvo's life are very few and throw little or no light of any significance on his literary interests. Of course, the usefulness of a writer's biography in studying his work, especially if he is a poet, can be and often is very limited. This once most famous romance of chivalry could have been the work of any one of many men of letters of the 1500s, since its subject was of universal interest to all the literate (and to many of the illiterate) of the period. Moreover, Montalvo's age still made a great cult of the pageantry (jousts, tourneys, processions, and so on) associated with chivalry. It was a time of reaffirmation of aristocratic values, while, in what must have been the second half of Montalvo's life, he saw the Spanish monarchy placed higher than he had known it, and its two chief representatives (Ferdinand and Isabella) become the object of veneration. This anonymity of subject of the *Amadís* is paralleled by the long tradition of the material itself, as will be shown in some detail in Chapter 3. It is surely more fruitful to try to suggest why the *Amadís* appeared when it did than to pursue fanciful ideas as to what kind of man Montalvo was.

What, however, is in fact known of Montalvo the man? Up until about forty years ago Garci Rodríguez de Montalvo (it is now clear that the alternative name, Garci Ordóñez de Montalvo, which caught on and was often repeated, in several post-1508 editions and references, was an error and has no basis in recorded fact) was only a name, although the 1508 edition refers to him as a native and an alderman (or "regidor") of Medina del Campo. (The same source also calls him "an honorable and virtuous knight.") We now know

13

that, in 1482, he was one of a hundred men from Medina who, after the capture of Alhama in the province of Granada from the Moors, were to be sent to police and guard this town. The same source calls Montalvo both an alderman and a gentleman ("Regidor, hidalgo"). Again, in 1490, our author is mentioned by full name as an alderman and his salary is given. Later documents speak of a Garci Rodríguez de Montalvo "the younger" ("el mozo"), who was the nephew of the novelist. It seems that by 1505 the latter had died, and there is evidence that by then a lawsuit was in progress as to who should inherit the title of alderman. A document of 1496 had also referred to a man with exactly the same names who had committed adultery, but it is held that this too must have been the author's nephew, chiefly on the grounds that the author of the *Amadís* would by then have been of advanced age! The nephew, it appears, died of the plague shortly after 1505. As late as 1519 there is evidence that the family municipal title was still being fought over by several descendants.

It is clear from the above account of his life (and it is all that is available to us) that Montalvo was a dignitary from a small European provincial city and that, in all probability, he spent most of his life there. At the same time, it should be added that Medina del Campo was a place especially favored by Isabella and her husband (the Queen died there in 1504), and that it became a royal residence at a time when Castile and Leon had no fixed capital (as distinct from the other Peninsular kingdoms with Barcelona, Saragossa, or Lisbon); further, it is to be thought of with Segovia and other towns in western Spain where there was spent much of the joint reign of two monarchs who are rightly regarded as the architects of imperial Spain. Medina del Campo became the great clearinghouse of the Spanish wool trade and the place of one of Europe's most famous fairs, while in the 1500s it was in consequence also an important center of printing (the 1545 edition of the *Amadís* came out there).

It has been plausibly argued that Montalvo attended the royal court in his native town and may there have got to know and even participate in the pageants of chivalry; indeed, he may have been stimulated by this experience to rewrite the *Amadís*. Much further than this it is not possible to go in speculating about our author's life and activities. Both the *Amadís* and the *Sergas de Esplandián* (*Deeds of Esplandian*) of 1510, Montalvo's continuation, speak of their author, and specifically of his beliefs and values, but at the level of fictional reality. It is doubtful to what extent the literary personality of a writer (even when it is, as here, deliberately projected into his work) is truly part of his biography. Let it be said once more that our novelist, whatever his literary gifts, and they have been regarded as very considerable, was in his *Amadís* reflecting the views of his age. His originality in doing so resulted in the production of a great classic of early European fiction, and yet Montalvo's real achievement was to have updated and given final form to inherited material that, as will be shown, was already well known to several generations of Spaniards.

While we do not know either the date of Montalvo's birth or that of his death, we can be reasonably certain that he lived most of his life in the period 1450–1500. He was a foot soldier in 1482 and thus at least a young adult, while there are references in his writings which indicate that he had some knowledge of the unsettled period before 1474, when Isabella and Ferdinand joined kingdoms, although this cannot be stated with any finality, since he might well have been quoting the views of others. Clear mention by Montalvo of the recapture of Granada, in the prologue to the *Amadís* and, indirectly, in Book I, Chapter 42 (a reference in the *Sergas de Esplandián*, however, seems to suggest that the campaign was not yet over), and of the achievements of the Catholic Monarchs and the probability of a first edition of the *Amadís* in 1496 (for which see again Chapter 3), would all indicate that his literary life falls within the last twenty years or so of the fifteenth century, perhaps within an even longer period. The civil wars of the previous reign of Isabella's brother, Henry IV, were followed, as every student of Spanish history knows, by the remarkable age of the Catholic Monarchs. The latter brought to an end in several ways the former instability, promoted new forms of government, and released fresh energies, thus placing their united kingdom in a position to emerge as the first modern nation-state and, through dynastic marriages, to dominate for a long time to come the military and political life of western Europe.

All this activity was built upon a rural economy of considerable strength—and Montalvo lived amid the towns and villages that created its wealth—and this in turn allowed Spain to become involved increasingly in European affairs and to undertake the discovery of the New World and all that this was to mean, although the impact of America on Spain was to come only after some considerable delay. Our novelist must then have witnessed much of the glamour and excitement of Isabelline Spain in its heyday.

In the field of culture, these years too saw great developments in literature and the arts, and this was also made possible through the vigorous economic and social life of the community. A most important development from which Montalvo's age and romance were greatly to benefit was, of course, the introduction of printing into Spain. The earliest attested examples, mostly the work of Germans, date from the 1470s and are from Segovia, Saragossa, Barcelona, Valencia, and Seville. A little later other cities in western Spain, Burgos, Valladolid, and Toledo, also appear to have acquired printing presses and produced their first books. Thus this very significant technological advance in the history of our Western culture was already well established in his own country when Montalvo's *Amadís* came out, either in the edition of 1496 (whose existence rests only on probability) or in the surviving first edition of 1508. This latter is printed in bold Gothic characters and illustrated with woodcuts. The arrival of the printing press in the Iberian Peninsula and its quick establishment there during the lifetime of Montalvo are other clear pointers to the general cultural activity that marked the 1400s and resulted in an ever-increasing demand for several kinds of literature, both in the vernaculars and in Latin.

It is hoped that a short account of the intellectual climate of the period 1400–1500, during which Montalvo came to maturity, will also help the reader to envisage the conditions in which he reworked the *Amadís*. One must assume, of course, that Montalvo had a knowledge of literature in his native language. Courtly and popular verse, for instance, he would certainly have known, since it and its recital constituted a very common staple of entertainment for all groups of educated people at that time. (As it happens, the *Amadís* contains only two pieces of verse, although one of them has caused much controversy in modern times, as we shall later see.) Montalvo's age not only produced a lot of verse in these two modes, but it is also from this period that we have some of its most famous collections (or *cancioneros*), such as the *Cancionero de Baena* (c. 1445–54), the earliest surviving, and others from the 1450s and 1460s, as well as the largest of all, the *Cancionero general* (1511) of Hernando del Castillo.

Poetry then also commonly included longer philosophical or moralistic, allegorical and descriptive forms, showing the influence of ancient models as well as of Dante and Petrarch. One of the outstanding figures in the poetry of the time (and indeed one of the patrons of literary culture generally) was the Marquis of Santillana (1406–54), who not only made original contributions to both lyrical and philosophical forms, but also composed the first critical and historical account of poetry in Castilian and other romance languages (in his *Carta-prohemio,* or *Letter-Prologue,* of c. 1449). The range of topics and attitudes that go to make up what we now refer to as the doctrine of courtly love form a vital part of the fictional prose as well as of the lyric verse of the time. Further, the mixing of prose and verse was also a feature of certain forms of fiction, and we shall see to what extent Montalvo's romance therefore partakes of the language and the content of much love poetry.

This age was also one when prose, of both the historical and imaginative varieties, was being used increasingly and with mature skill. It is, of course, now fully recognized that the so-called Renaissance (as it concerns literature) did not suddenly happen but that, even if one can put an approximate date on it, it was, rather than a rebirth, a development and a maturing from earlier achievements. Thus one finds (in verse and prose) both survivals in taste and new experiments side by side, and indeed the *Amadís* itself, as left to us by Montalvo, is a striking example of old material refashioned and made into something which was to have an unusual power of survival and influence. In something like the same way the prevalent European taste for didactic prose, now with a markedly pessimistic note (due in part no doubt to memories of the Black Death and other such calamities during the second half of the 1300s), produced such a remarkable work as the *Corbacho* (1438) by Alfonso Martínez de Toledo, archpriest of Talavera; this attacks the sin of lust and also has some of the liveliness and realism of a good sermon.

Much other didactic prose in Spanish belongs to this period: one example is a last survival of thirteenth-century *exemplum* (moral tale) literature, the *Libro de los gatos (Book of the Cats,* 1400–20), a collection of animal tales of different origins, although it is a version of a similar work by the Englishman Odo of Cheriton (d. 1247). Another such example of earlier fictional prose is the *Libro de los exenplos por A.B.C.,* in fact the largest collection of this kind, by Clemente Sánchez de Vercial (d. c. 1434). Many other works in prose include both religious and secular treatises by such well-

known figures as Alfonso de Cartagena (1384–1456). Hernando de
Talavera (1428–1507), the first archbishop of Granada after its recapture in 1492, and Diego de Valera (1412–88?) There is in addition the *Visión delectable* (late 1430s) by Alfonso de la Torre: this
allegorical work, again recalling earlier tastes and using well-known
sources, was copied out and reprinted and even translated as late as
1623. The works of Juan de Lucena (d. 1506) should also be mentioned: these include a dialogue on the blessed life and an epistle in
praise of Queen Isabella. Montalvo's active life as a writer coincided
with two of the first works on the Spanish language, Alfonso de
Palencia's *Universal vocabulario en latín y romance* (1490), and the
much more famous *Gramática sobre la lengua castellana* (1492), of
the humanist and tutor to the royal family, Antonio de Nebrija.
Historical prose in the 1400s ran both to chronicles and to biographies, and it was also a period of continuing translation, chiefly
from Latin, Italian, and French, of works of many kinds of literature. Attention should again be drawn to the profusion of writings
and to their considerable variety as two characteristics of the
century's literary activities.

As far as the literary works closest to the *Amadís* are concerned,
that is, the Spanish versions of chivalric romance, these for the most
part appear to belong to the early and the middle part of the
fourteenth century, and some have come down to us in fragments
(we shall later refer to the earlier history of the *Amadís*, of which the
earliest recorded mention is c. 1350). It is now thought that the
prose versions (in Castilian, Catalan, and Portuguese) derive from
the so-called Post-Vulgate form of the material in French, which was
at one time attributed to Robert de Boron (thirteenth century). In
Montalvo's own lifetime two full translations appeared in Spain, the
Baladro del sabio Merlín (The Cry of the Wizard Merlin), in 1498,
and the *Tristán de Leonís* (1501). These and other Spanish versions
of the earlier chivalric material (Arthurian, Carolingian, and other)
now made the romance of chivalry, thanks to the recent invention of
printing, the most popular form of fiction throughout several
generations. This is also a convenient place to refer to the recent
discovery (in 1955) of the *Amadís* fragments (to be discussed later):
these are from a manuscript probably copied c. 1420 and constitute
the first firm evidence of an earlier text of the romance (and they are
in Spanish); the fragments also show that Montalvo in fact cut down
rather than expanded his inherited material.

The 1400s (and the early 1500s) saw a profusion of other romances of chivalry, using material from a variety of sources, and these also continued to be popular in the succeeding century. Certain works drew on history and legend as well as on purely fictional material: the *Historia del abad Don Juan de Montemayor* (c. 1500) deals with Christian sacrifice in a Portuguese town invaded by the Moors in the tenth century, and the much more ambitious *Crónica sarracina* (1499), of Pedro del Corral, collects into a developed novelistic framework the story of Roderick, last king of the Visigoths, his reign and his tragic overthrow. This work shows the influence, in subject matter and methods, of all kinds of contemporary fiction (the primitive *Amadís* could well have suggested some episodes). Other novels with a vaguely historical background are: the *Historia del noble Vespesiano emperador de Roma* (c. 1490), which mixes early Christian history and chivalric fiction, and is a translation from the French, and the *Historia de La Poncella de Francia* (1512), a free version of the life of Joan of Arc. The *Historia de Enrique Fi de Oliva* (1498), probably of remote French origin, and the *Historia del emperador Carlomagno y de los doce Pares de Francia* (published in 1525 but translated from an earlier French romance) both show descent from the early Carolingian epic cycle. Purely legendary in source, but of short dimension and of generally contemporary settings, are the following: the *Historia de los nobles cavalleros Oliveros de Castilla y Artús de Algarbe* (1499), again translated from the French, despite the Hispanic setting; *La espantosa y maravillosa vida de Roberto el Diablo* (1509), also translated from a French original; the *Historia de los enamorados Flores y Blancaflor* (1512, but probably from the late fifteenth century): this is of unknown sources, but is the Spanish version of a legend of very wide diffusion in medieval Europe. Several other translations from the French include the *Historia del muy valiente Clamades y de la linda Claramonda* (1480); the *Historia de la linda Magalona y Pierres de Provenza* (1519, but published in French in 1478), and the rather promiscuous romance, the *Historia del rey Canamor y de Turián su hijo* (1509), which owed much to Breton sources and appears to be an authentic Spanish work.

The 1400s also witnessed the rise of a new form of fiction, the sentimental novel, derived from the poetic tradition of courtly love (as found in the *cancioneros*), from the sentimental fiction of Boccaccio and others, and, in places, from the chivalric romance itself.

It could be a mixture of prose and verse (as indicated above), but for the most part it took the form of an intense analysis of feelings with limited external narration or description. What there is of the latter, however, depicts a society of chivalric habits and conventions. The form became firmly established in Spain and may well have reflected and even inspired the courtly behavior and mores of the period. The best-remembered examples are *El siervo libre de amor* by Juan Rodríguez del Padrón or de la Cámara (d. after 1440), the famous *Cárcel de amor* by Diego de San Pedro (1492), and *Grimalte y Gradissa* and *Grisel y Mirabella*, both of c. 1495 and both by Juan de Flores.

The sentimental novel has, it will have been seen, more than one point of similarity with the *Amadís*, which also makes much use of the despairs and hopes of sexual love and of its consequences on the lives of the characters, although, as will be observed, the *Amadís* also represents the triumph of true love. Further, the closely written style of the sentimental novel is in general contrast to the looser and more flowing prose of most of the *Amadís* and of the romance of chivalry as a form. Reference should also be made here to a distinct novelistic form, which partakes rather more of the romance of chivalry but which also contains much of the same kind of psychological introspection as the sentimental novel. This developed in Catalan and is represented first by *Curial e Güelfa* (written some time between 1435 and 1462), which relates the love and the knightly adventures of the hero and also makes use of recognizable natural backgrounds in Europe and North Africa, and often refers to real events and persons, for example from the contemporary court of Burgundy. The second and much more famous example is the *Tirant lo blanc* (much praised, it will be recalled, by Cervantes) by Martorell and Galba, first published in 1490. The *Tirant* also moves in a world and a setting from which there is absent the fantasy of the *Amadís*, although much of its concern is with chivalry; it is a more ambitious work than *Curial e Güelfa* and gives many memorable scenes from contemporary court life and of individual combat and large-scale battles set in a variety of places from England to Greece, these last also reflecting the contemporary Turkish threat to Christendom (as, indeed, it is held, do the adventures of Amadís and Esplandián). Both these Catalan classics thus combine in an original way the circumstantial observation common to historical prose with the obsessive analysis of erotic experience typical of courtly love. Both novels, which have been called "chivalric novels" to distinguish them from the books of chivalry proper, again underline the vogue for chivalric literature in the period and also recall the prevalence of chivalric practices in contemporary society, which will be mentioned later in this chapter.

Finally, but by no means least in this survey of literature during the 1400s, there comes one of Spain's great classics, the *Tragicomedia de Calisto y Melibea* (universally known as the *Celestina*, from one of its main characters, the bawd of this name). This first appeared in print in 1499 at Burgos and is the work of Fernando de Rojas (he was a native of the province of Toledo, and his library contained, according to a contemporary document, copies of the *Cancionero general*, the *Visión delectable*, the *Cárcel de amor*, and the *Amadís*, thus providing in a way not frequently recorded some idea of the reading tastes of a man of his age). This justly famous novel in dramatic form is a most original fusion of several literary modes and makes use of subjects taken from courtly love and contemporary ascetic thought, while also combining with great artistry contrasting social types. It is a triumph of early realism and penetrating psychological study based on the tragic end of passionate love and criminal intrigue. The *Celestina* was to equal only the *Amadís*, as an example of fifteenth-century fiction, in its wide and continuing influence up to the Golden Age and beyond.

Montalvo, then, flourished at a time when the different currents of medieval European culture merged to produce a rich vernacular literature, which his romance reflects and with which it has several affinities. The *Amadís* can thus be seen as sharing the manners and the values of fifteenth-century Spanish society, while at the same time, like many other examples of contemporary literature, it must be seen as a survival of a form that arose at a much earlier period. Montalvo, however, seems to have adapted it to the peculiar demands of late-fifteenth-century taste, by, for example, making additions of moralistic material, chiefly in the shape of authorial exhortations or of sermons spoken by the characters. Thus the *Amadís* includes several significant passages on fortune and on man's part in it, on God's dispensation, on good and evil in general, and on a prince's duties and responsibilities. Some of these passages are prophetic in nature and function while others simply serve to comment on what has already happened. They indicate clearly

Montalvo's use of contemporary preoccupations and their didactic expression in much of the literature of the time, and they can also be said to echo the new religious fervor and public-spiritedness characteristic of Isabelline Spain. This period of the early Renaissance is naturally marked by an interest in humanism, although the latter is frequently modified by the Spanish emphasis on the traditional Christian views of man and of his world—thus the greater preference for the allegorical and moralistic works of Dante and Petrarch rather than the more daring productions of later Italian humanists. This peculiarly Spanish fusion of the old and the new can also be strikingly illustrated by the religious humanism of the great churchman and statesman, Francisco Jiménez de Cisneros, founder of the University of Alcalá (1510), where he presided over the production of Europe's first printed polyglot Bible.

Montalvo and his contemporaries had at their disposal a Castilian vernacular which had acquired considerable maturity as a language of literature. The variety of forms of literature in fifteenth-century Spain called forth a corresponding range of styles. Thus in verse one passes from the unadorned but subtle style of courtly poetry to the equally mannered but daring rhetoric of Juan de Mena (1411–56), whose Latinizing experiments with vocabulary and syntax anticipate much later practice. Prose developed different styles as the occasion required, for declamation, reported speech, dialogue, description, or narration, while the sentimental novel made use of a tight and witty prose, recalling that of courtly verse. The fluent, even loose, paratactical prose which fitted the needs of historical works finds a clear echo in the romances and it is not at all accidental that Montalvo frequently refers to his work as a history. This, of course, helps to preserve the illusion, created in the prologues to Books I and IV, when he states that the *Amadís* is in fact by another and was brought to Spain and translated by himself (Cervantes was also to use this trick in *Don Quixote*). But the language of the *Amadís* in fact has many points of similarity with that of the chronicles, although the novel also uses a variety of styles to suit its changing material and is generally written with more liveliness and vividness than many historical records of the period. (See above for references to certain novels of chivalry and their connection with the historical record.) Both the language of verse and that of prose were to undergo further developments and to reach a greater level of sophistication during the following century, largely in the direction of greater suppleness and variety, under the constant imitation of Latin models. It must again be stressed, however, that the *Amadís*, and the *Celestina*, were to continue to influence this new era of growth and achievement more than many other works of their period. In fact, the *Amadís* started a vogue for romances of chivalry that was to create one of the most insistent demands for printed literature throughout the 1500s. Thus it can be said that the language and the content of medieval fiction were to make a far-reaching contribution to new areas of imaginative endeavor and to stimulate new forms of the novel into the nineteenth century itself.

To round off this summary, special mention should be made of a very direct connection between Montalvo's *Amadís* and the readers for whom it was intended. This is to be found in the actual habits of his time when in fact chivalry still played a large part in the collective life of the ruling classes. This society took seriously the ideals and the deeds of knights, and spent much time and money in encouraging their demonstration. First, it should be said that our knowledge of this strong survival of a kind of chivalric activity down to early modern times comes not alone from the *Amadís* itself and the other romances published at the same time (and these are a clear indication of a demand and of its accompanying taste), but also from the widespread recording of the deeds of actual knights. Thus the anonymous chronicles of the Frenchman Jacques de Lalaing, whose stories read like the fictional ones of the contemporary chivalric novel, namely, the *Petit Jehan de Saintré* (c. 1456), but which are in fact historical accounts. Similarly the Spanish *Libro del passo honroso (Book of the Passage of Honor)*, by Pero Rodríguez de Lena—first published in 1588 and in abbreviated form by Juan de Pineda—tells the true story of the young knight Suero de Quiñones, who in 1434, with the permission of King John II of Castile, threw down a challenge to all comers by holding a bridge over the River Órbigo in the province of Leon, and on the road to the famous center of pilgrimage at Santiago de Compostela. This challenge also took the form of a tribute to the knight's lady: nine companions helped him to hold out for a month and to fight no fewer than sixty-eight knights, both Spanish and foreign. In these encounters one man died and others on both sides were wounded. This, the best-remembered performance of its kind in Spain, was by no means uncommon, and may itself have been organized in answer to another one arranged by Prince Henry of Aragon in challenge to

Castilian knights. Indeed, the Spaniards who came to fight Suero included several from eastern Spain. It is also likely that Suero was patronized in his endeavors by the powerful royal favorite, Álvaro de Luna. Many other cases are recorded from fifteenth-century Spain (in for example the *Crónica de Juan II*, first published 1517) of knights who traveled far and wide to acquire fame through valor, while many foreign knights visited Spain for the same purpose. The encounters themselves were also at times organized in order to seek revenge or amends or for the ransoming of prisoners.

Montalvo must have known and read of such activities and indeed he may well have witnessed some of them. His society, which, in a mixture of solemn playacting and serious sport, indulged its taste for the spectacular and rechanneled the older aggressiveness of feudal times, thus produced a kind of applied literature. The books of chivalry often reflected an authentic social reality which itself provided material for novelists. It is an unusual case of osmosis with novelists and knights alike imbued with literary fantasy, thus making literature and life interact, and it recalls the later and long-lasting acting out of pastoral scenes in *fêtes champêtres* as late as the 1700s, although the latter were strictly either charades or semidramatic entertainment. In the 1400s chivalry was very much in the air and its fictional representation in great demand (people even took to calling their children and their pets after Arthurian heroes). The *Amadís* was then a very natural product of a society which used its literature to keep alive the ideals of a way of life institutionalized a long time before, or, as it has been stated recently, the romance of chivalry formed in a way a kind of substitute for the fulfillment of ideals which were constantly broken in practice. We have also seen above romances like the *Tirant lo blanc*, which drew on names, events, and settings from contemporary history and society and thus added fresh stimulus to the vogue for chivalric literature and increased its level of acceptability. The 1500s continued to use the *Amadís* and its like to interpret and to redefine behavior in a courtly society, although one should also make it clear that the manual of social conduct made up from extracts from Montalvo's romance encouraged the emulation of the milder and more intimate aspects of the knight's way of life, as we shall see later.[1]

The Amadís de Gaula: *An Outline*

M ONTALVO'S romance, *Amadís de Gaula*, is a long work, its length, however, being by no means untypical of its age and of its reading habits. It is divided into four *libros* (books), and it runs to a total of 132 chapters, which themselves are disposed as follows: Book I, 44; Book II, 21; Book III, 16; Book IV, 51. Book I also has a short but important prologue, while the first chapter is unnumbered and is headed simply "Here begins the First Book," the true Chapter 2 being numbered as the first. Book II has no prologue but it does open in the same way with an unnumbered chapter, which, however, supplies the background concerning the Ínsola Firme, and the second chapter then takes up the numbered sequence from Book I. Book III has the same opening arrangement as Book II; Book IV has a prologue telling how this book was found hidden in a tomb near Constantinople and brought to Spain, as related in the prologue to Book I (it should be mentioned that the common view is that Book IV is mostly Montalvo's own invention); the prologue also states that Book IV makes more mention of Esplandián and of his glorious future. Further, the disparity in the number of chapters as between one book and another can also be seen, to a certain extent, if one considers the division by pages (the edition used for this calculation and throughout this monograph is the standard one by E. B. Place, for which see our bibliography; in this edition, based on that of 1508, the chapter numbers run throughout the four volumes): Book I, 354; Book II, 229; Book III, 260; Book IV, 387.

The slight disparity between the number of chapters and that of pages can easily be explained by the changing length of the chapters (these tend to become shorter in Book IV, perhaps another indication that Montalvo has reworked and augmented his inherited material). The narrative pace of the *Amadís* is to a considerable extent due to the division of this material into reasonably short chapters which thus keep alive the reader's interest and also allow him to organize his reading of what, as has been said, is a very long story. This is, of course, a very obvious way of dealing structurally with an extended area of fiction, and it was to be generally followed by Cervantes and some of his own followers. In the case of the *Amadís*, it can be pointed out that longer chapters are given, for example, to the episodes concerning Amadís when he was in the wilderness as Beltenebrós (Book II), or during his adventures in another form of exile, as the Knight of the Green Sword in eastern Europe (Book III). On the other hand, Book IV contains the drawn-out events of the final battles between Amadís and his allies, on the one hand, and Lisuarte, the emperor of Rome, and theirs, on the other, and yet this book is mostly divided, as already stated, into short chapters. (There are, however, some long chapters here too, as, for example, those dealing with Amadís's final adventures.)

The necessary conclusion is that this kind of narrative, loose and potentially burgeoning as it is, can be subdivided one way or another. There are, of course, other narrative devices used to help and attract the reader, that is, other than the simple division into chapters. Thus throughout much of the novel the author, both within a chapter and at the end of one, moves from one adventure or setting to another and later returns to it, in this way spinning out more than one narrative thread at the same time, as it were. This is an old technique of the early medieval romance, known to modern scholarship as interweaving, or *entrelacement*, and is characteristic in particular of the later Arthurian material, from which the *Amadís* is clearly derived, and in which medieval conceptions of proportion are illustrated. The difference, and it is a most important one, between the latter and its models, is that the *Amadís* develops a real overall (if circular) pattern through which the story rises to climaxes and is eventually rounded off with the final triumphs of the hero and the consequent settlements (Book IV also makes a beginning, if tentative, of the adventures of Amadís's son, Esplandián, which are to outshine those of his progenitor and make up the *Sergas*, or Book V). The denouement, then, is much more typical of the modern or neoclassical aesthetic view of the structure of a work of literature (it may be recalled that Malory did something similar for the English-speaking world in his rearrangement of Arthurian material). We do not, of course, know for sure how much of this refurbishing is the work of Montalvo or whether the process had begun earlier. We are reasonably certain that he made a major contribution to the process, not alone by inventing new fictional material, but also by adding further to the variety of the narrative with his authorial and other moralistic comments and interventions. Further examination of Montalvo's handling of his inherited material will be made in Chapter 4.

This is perhaps the place to provide a summary of the plot of the *Amadís* in which many of the subsidiary adventures (which cause much of the interweaving) will be omitted, while the chief characters and the main threads of the story will be singled out, and certain comments on the narrative added within square brackets:

Book I. In his prologue Montalvo considers how much more those ancients, concerned with recording events of arms both for the information and the wonder of posterity, would have had to tell had they coincided in time with the holy conquest of Granada. The great prince who carried it out would be worthy of their highest praise, and he and his queen are in any case to be placed above the emperors of old because their cause was God's while the latters' was to obtain the world's reward. Livy deserves credit for telling in detail of the valor and the deeds of the Romans. Others, however, in speaking of the heroes of the Trojan war or even of Godfrey of Boulogne and the First Crusade, go beyond the historical facts in their accounts, while others yet again have written purely fictional histories. We should take from all these works both moral examples and teaching suitable for our soul's salvation. With all this in mind, Montalvo has corrected the three books of Amadís, purging them of their corrupt state, and he has transferred (translated) and emended Book IV together with the *Sergas de Esplandián* (that is, the deeds of Amadís's son). This last work and Book IV were discovered in a tomb near Constantinople and brought to Spain by a Hungarian merchant and translated (transcribed) with great difficulty. The five books, although for long regarded rather as fiction than history, are now accompanied by most uplifting examples and teaching for people of all ages, and Mother Church has dictated Montalvo's choice of such material.

The story begins not many years after Our Lord's Passion, with the arrival of King Perión of Gaul in Little Britain, whose Christian king, Garínter, he meets by chance in the woods but whom he had come to see. When Perión meets Garínter's younger daughter

Elisena, at that time living almost like a nun, he falls in love with her at once [as their son is to do with Oriana in similar circumstances], and soon, with the assistance of Darioleta, Elisena's companion, their love is consummated. [Their union is presented as one of true love and tokens and promises are given; thus we have the first example in the novel of the marriage of vows, or secret marriage; the case of Amadís's and Oriana's subsequent ceremony is much longer delayed]. Perión leaves Little Britain and Elisena gives birth secretly to Amadís, whom she is compelled with equal secrecy to dispatch in a chest on the open sea, but with the ring Perión gave her and his sword, together with a letter calling our hero by his first nickname, "Sin Tiempo" ("Without Time," since it was not thought he could survive), but also declaring that he is a king's son. Amadís is rescued by the Scottish knight Gandales, who now rears him with his own son, Gandalín [the latter is to become Amadís's most loyal squire]. Here we have the first appearance of the good fairy, Urganda la Desconocida ("The Unknown," because she appears in several forms and is thus difficult to know), who foretells for Gandales the great future of Amadís.

The latter is in due course presented at the court of King Languines of Scotland. (Perión and Elisena have two other children, Galaor, a son, and Melicia, a daughter.) Lisuarte, newly king of Great Britain, leaves his daughter Oriana in the care of Languines, and Amadís, now a young page, together with his cousin Mabilia and the Doncella de Denamarcha (Damsel of Denmark), is allocated to serve her. Amadís and Oriana fall deeply in love and he is made a knight by Perión, his unknown father, who is visiting Scotland. Amadís's first adventures prove his skill and valor, for which Urganda gives him a lance. His brother Galaor, carried off when an infant by a giant and given to a hermit to rear, is now also a young man and learns that he too is a king's son, while being trained by the giant as a knight. Oriana, accompanied by Mabilia, rejoins her father Lisuarte in London. Amadís, joined by Agrajes (his cousin and the son of Languines), arrives at his father's court and, with Agrajes and Perión, defeats Abiés, King of Ireland. Amadís receives a letter from Oriana to join her and, now recognized by his parents, he sets out and lands at Bristoya (Bristol). On his way to Vindilisora (Windsor) he meets up with Urganda and Galaor, the latter also on his way to become a knight at Lisuarte's court, and, before knowing who he is, Amadís dubs him with Urganda's support, and a gift of a new sword. Amadís later leaves Lisuarte's court at Vindilisora in search for Galaor, but he is enchanted by the evil magician Arcaláus, who brings the false news of his death to Lisuarte.

Eventually Amadís is freed and comes to Vindilisora with Galaor, and they join with Lisuarte and others to go to a great assembly in London, where all the knights swear to protect ladies and damsels. Later Lisuarte and his retinue are treacherously captured and imprisoned by Arcaláus, who hopes to make Barsinán of Sansueña king of Great Britain. Amadís then proceeds to defeat Arcaláus and free Oriana from his clutches. Amadís and Oriana finally consummate their love.

Galaor meanwhile in his turn has released Lisuarte from Arcaláus's castle, but this did not occur before Barsinán tried to become king or before he was defeated by Amadís; Lisuarte then ordered him to be burned alive. The *cortes* (assembly) in London lasted twelve days and were attended by a vast concourse of knights and ladies.

Amadís, accompanied by Galaor and Agrajes, then fulfills his promise to avenge Queen Briolanja of Sobradisa by defeating her father's murderers and restoring her to her kingdom. This causes the beginnings of deep jealousy in Oriana since Briolanja falls passionately in love with Amadís, although the latter remains completely faithful to Oriana (the author here relates the alternative accounts of this episode, according to which a Prince Alfonso of Portugal had the story changed so that Briolanja imprisoned Amadís until he should give her a child, and, when Oriana saw that her lover was dying of hunger, she gave him permission to make love to Briolanja). Amadís and his companions are given rest and lavish entertainment after the defeat of Abíseos, the usurper, and his sons. Galaor discovers that one of his combatants is in fact his and Amadís's half brother, Florestán, son of Perión and the daughter of the Count of Selandia (Zeeland). [Florestán is to become an inseparable fellow-warrior of his two brothers].

Book II. First, and because events in Book IV also stem from it, the Ínsola Firme (Firm Island) and its origins are here described: Apolidón, son of a king of Greece, won the island from an evil giant and he and his beloved Grimanesa lived there in great happiness and made of it a place of beauty and many riches. When he was later asked to become emperor of Greece, Grimanesa persuaded him to

make sure that the island should always be ruled by a true knight
and lover. Thus they constructed the Arco de los Leales Amadores
(Loyal Lovers' Arch), under which only faithful lovers would pass, to
the sweet sounds of a trumpet played by a bronze figure; otherwise
the trumpet would expel them with smoke, flames, and a dreadful
noise. Beyond the arch they made two images of themselves, and a
bright jasper stone as well as a tall iron pillar; in a room, on the door
of which true lovers' names would appear, Apolidón placed two
other pillars, of stone and bronze, each with inscriptions for brave
knights and for the one who is better than Apolidón and for a lady
more beautiful than Grimanesa; he who entered the room would
also become lord of the island. These and other tests were to be
undertaken by Apolidón's successor and his virtuous companions,
after which the enchantment involved would end. Meanwhile
Apolidón left the Ínsola Firme in charge of a governor.

Amadís, his brothers, and Agrajes, on the way back to Lisuarte's
court, are by chance taken to the island where Isanjo, the then
governor, shows them its wonders. They all try to win the tests but
only Amadís succeeds, as a true lover and as the new lord of Ínsola
Firme, where he and his companions are now well received and
feasted; this takes place one hundred years after Apolidón has left it.
Good fortune now begins to turn against Amadís when he receives
Oriana's letter accusing him of abandoning her for Briolanja.
Amadís's distress is beyond measure and he wanders off into the
wilds, where, after more adventures, he retires as a hermit, with the
name of Beltenebrós, to the island fastness of Peña Pobre (Poor
Rock), until he should win back Oriana's favor. She, when she hears
of his grief, is herself overcome and sends a new letter to him to
Scotland, thinking he has fled there. Another knight, Guilán el
Cuidador ("he who takes care") finds Amadís's shield and arms and
brings them to court and Oriana's anguish is increased. Corisanda,
searching for her lover Florestán, visits the Peña Pobre and then
goes to the court where her story of Beltenbrós makes Mabilia
believe that he is Amadís. The Doncella de Denamarcha is then
dispatched with a letter, asking forgiveness for Oriana, who hopes
Amadís will join her in her castle of Miraflores. Amadís, overjoyed,
sets off.

At court Corisanda and Florestán are reunited, and Lisuarte gets
his little daughter Leonoreta (who is to become empress of Rome) to
sing for Galaor and his companions a song which Amadís had

composed for her [this, as will be seen, was to be used in the argument concerning the supposed Portuguese origin of the *Amadís*, and it is the only other piece of verse in the romance apart from Amadís's song of complaint when in Peña Pobre, a few chapters before]. Amadís, on his way to Miraflores, has several adventures. Apolidón's nephew, the old page Macandón, later made a knight by Amadís, then appears at court, and it is arranged that Amadís and Oriana should come in disguise to pass the tests of true love by winning the green sword and the headdress of miraculous flowers respectively. Further adventures ensue and Briolanja visits Oriana at Miraflores. Urganda, in her magic ship, visits the king to warn Lisuarte to keep the love of his knights, and to remind them of prophecies fulfilled and of troubles yet to come, in all of which she praises in particular the valor of Amadís. Lisuarte, although well and loyally served by Amadís and his companions, now listens to the envious and slanderous courtiers and adherents of Falangrís, Lisuarte's brother and predecessor, namely, Brocadán and Gandandel; they are jealous for the preferment of their own sons in place of Amadís and his companions, who have come only lately to court. These courtiers poison the king's mind and make him refuse Amadís's request to pardon Madasima (daughter of the giant Famongomadán, defeated and killed by Amadís), and give her to Galvanes, uncle of Agrajes, as his wife, with the Island of Mongaça as a dowry. Amadís, offended, decides to leave the court. Oriana reluctantly accepts his decision, and he and his brothers and others go to the Ínsola Firme. Oriana hears how Briolanja had also passed the tests of a loyal lover. Amadís now sends twelve of his knights to defend Madasima and other damsels under threat of death from Lisuarte. They win the day against twelve others including Brocadán and Gandandel, to Lisuarte's displeasure, and to the joy of Oriana and Mabilia, and Madasima and her companions are freed.

Book III. The opposing hosts, and navies, of Lisuarte and Amadís contend for the Island of Mongaça, with victory for Amadís's men and the installation there of Madasima and her husband, Galvanes sin Tierra ("without land"). Amadís and Galaor arrive in Gaul where their parents joyfully receive them, but Galaor returns to Lisuarte to whose service he is pledged. Norandel, Lisuarte's natural son, is, unrecognized by him, made a knight. Oriana gives birth to her and Amadís's son, who is found to have imprinted on his chest some

white and seven red mysterious letters. When being taken by the
Doncella de Denamarcha and her brother Durín to be reared at
Miraflores, the child is seized by a lioness, which, however, lets the
boy be rescued by the hermit Nasciano, who in turn gives him to his
sister and her husband to rear until he can teach him to read.
Nasciano reads the white letters (in Latin) as "Esplandián," and thus
he baptizes him.

Lisuarte, after besieging Galvanes and Madasima, agrees, on
Galaor's pleading, to leave them their island, although under his
lordship. Amadís becomes restless and sad, because of idleness and
absence from Oriana, in Gaul, but he then joins his father and
brothers to fight for Lisuarte against King Arábigo, a friend of Arcaláus, and his allies. On their way home to Gaul they are held for a
time by Arcaláus in an enchanted castle.

Amadís decides now to visit foreign lands in search of adventures
to prove his valor anew. When Esplandián is four years old, he and
his foster mother's son pass into Nasciano's care and they learn to
hunt with the lioness. Amadís, now known as the Knight of the
Green Sword [see above] or of the Dwarf (who accompanied him),
and, with Gandalín his squire, is to spend five years away from Gaul
and the Ínsola Firme. After winning fame in Germany, he proceeds
to Bohemia to help King Trafinor and his son Grasandor and cousin
Galtines against El Patín (the Little Duck), emperor of Rome, who
also wishes to marry Oriana, and in this he succeeds, while Trafinor
promises to help Amadís on a later occasion. Lisuarte and his retinue while hunting find Esplandián and Nasciano and have the boy
brought to court where he is given to his mother Oriana to rear.
Oriana confesses to Nasciano her love for Amadís and reveals that
Esplandián is her son, and Nasciano, after reproving her, accepts
her explanation of their vows and absolves her.

Amadís grieves for Oriana but is comforted by Gandalín. Now two
years away from Gaul they arrive at the seaport (near Greece) of
Trafinor's niece Grasinda, who has heard of Amadís's valor. After
getting him to promise to return within a year, she gives him a ship
and sends with him the great physician Elisabad and they have
several adventures among the islands of Rumania. They then come
to the Ínsola del Diablo (Island of the Devil), the abode of the
fearsome monster, the Endriago, who was both the fruit of incest
and the killer of its own father and mother. After a frightful en-

counter, Amadís, grievously wounded, kills the beast and is himself cured of his awful wounds by Elisabad. The emperor of Constantinople, greatly indebted for this deliverance, has Amadís and his companions brought by ship to his court and there feasted and honored. Amadís, although he has to tell who is the present lord of the Ínsola Firme, refuses to drop his disguise, and he hears about the history of Grimanesa's ring, which the emperor's daughter Leonorina gives him and which Esplandián is later to restore to the princess. [Here we get the first mention by Montalvo of *Las sergas de Esplandián*].

Amadís sees the wonders of Constantinople but still pines for the absent Oriana. El Patín sends his cousin Salustanquidio and a great company to Lisuarte's court to ask for Oriana's hand. Florestán successfully challenges several Roman knights and takes their shields to the Ínsola Firme. Amadís, still using the name of Knight of the Green Sword, returns, as promised, to Grasinda, who now requests him to take her to Lisuarte's court to support her challenge as the most beautiful of ladies; Amadís agrees but, for obvious reasons, reluctantly. Together with two loyal companions, Bruneo de Bonamar and Angriote de Estraváus, they set out by ship for Great Britain. El Patín's niece, Queen Sardamira of Sardinia, who accompanied Salustanquidio, now visits Queen Brisena and Oriana and tells them of Amadís's great deeds in Bohemia. Lisuarte and Galaor disagree over the former's plans to marry Oriana to the emperor of Rome and to leave Great Britain to Leonoreta. Amadís, Grasinda, and the others reach the open sea off the coast of Spain, and, as they approach Great Britain, he asks them all to refer to him only as the Caballero Griego (the Greek Knight). They arrive at Lisuarte's court, where the king continues to ignore advice and pleas and makes arrangements for Oriana to marry El Patín.

At the same time Grasinda's challenge is taken up; in this Amadís, as the Greek Knight, wins a great victory against the proud Romans, for whose lives Esplandián intervenes, after which he shows his father his name inscribed on his chest. Amadís and his friends now prepare to attack the fleet taking Oriana to Rome. Stubborn to the end and deaf to all advice, Lisuarte sends off his stricken daughter. Amadís now reveals his true identity to Grasinda, whom he leaves with Isanjo in the Ínsola Firme, and sets off with his faithful followers in a fleet to meet Salustanquidio. In the sea battle which follows the latter is killed and Oriana, Mabilia, Sardamira, and others are rescued, and Amadís determines to take them all to the Ínsola Firme.

Book IV. The prologue speaks of the discovery after many years of this book in the tomb—as mentioned at the beginning of Book I—and in particular of the life of Esplandián, his faultless youth and his total dedication to God and the Faith, even when he becomes emperor of Constantinople, as well as king of Great Britain and Gaul, administering Christian justice and in all things observing the demands of religion. This late discovery now helps his life to serve as an example to all to act virtuously and to fight the infidel, thus winning for them everlasting life.

Amadís, Oriana, and many others, including prisoners and spoils, set sail for the Ínsola Firme where Grasinda with a great company receives them all. Amadís, recalling his duty as a Christian knight, gets the agreement of everyone, including Oriana, that an attempt be made to achieve peace and harmony with Lisuarte, and the Irishman Quadragante and the Spaniard Brián de Monjaste are sent off as ambassadors. Grasinda offers to stay with Oriana and to send Elisabad to the emperor of Constantinople and to her own land to ask for help for Amadís when this is needed. Similar messages are sent to Queen Briolanja, to Perión, and to Languines of Scotland and the queen of Ireland, as well as to King Trafinor of Bohemia.

Meanwhile, Mabilia reveals to Amadís that Esplandián is his son, while Oriana sends a letter with Durín to her mother Brisena to urge Lisuarte to make peace. The latter, after much thought, decides to declare war on Amadís and company for killing Salustanquidio and taking Oriana, and he now too collects his forces. Arcaláus, King Arábigo, and Barsinán's son of the same name decide to take advantage of the coming struggle in order to take revenge on both sides, and thus they also collect forces from near and far. Briolanja also goes to the Ínsola Firme, where she is received as queen by Oriana, Grasinda, and Mabilia. Amadís and his companions regretfully decide that war with Lisuarte is now the only honorable course, and their widespread appeals for help are answered. Lisuarte too sends Guilán to Rome where El Patín promises to come to his help, as others do, although Galvanes, now Lisuarte's vassal as lord of Mongaça, asks to be excused from fighting his nephew Agrajes and the latter's cousin Amadís. Forces on both sides are drawn up and counted: Amadís's and Perión's on the Ínsola Firme, Lisuarte's and El Patín's and others at Vindilisora. Oriana is comforted and hopes for victory for Amadís.

Meanwhile Arcaláus and Arábigo and their hosts get ready to take advantage of their enemies. Lisuarte and El Patín set out and Amadís decides to avoid an encounter with Lisuarte, as Oriana's father and as his former lord. Two great battles take place each lasting for one day: Amadís kills El Patín and things go badly for Lisuarte, but Amadís, out of love for Oriana, calls a truce of two days to bury the many dead and heal the wounded. Before the conflict is renewed, the holy man Nasciano, with Oriana's support, intervenes with Lisuarte and tells him that Amadís and Oriana are married [again we have a clear reference to the secret marriage], and that Esplandián is their son. Nasciano, now accompanied by Esplandián, carries Lisuarte's offer of peace to Amadís, who joyfully accepts it, as does Perión, and both Esplandián's father and grandfather are amazed at his handsome appearance. Thus Urganda's prophecy that Nasciano and Esplandián would act as peacemakers is fulfilled.

King Arábigo with Arcaláus, however, decides to carry out his plan and attacks Lisuarte on his way back to his town of Lubaina, where he is besieged and heavily defeated. Esplandián informs Amadís, who, with all his company—less Galaor who is ill and is pledged to Lisuarte—comes to the latter's aid just in time, defeats the enemy, and imprisons Arcaláus, Arábigo, and their followers. Arquisil meanwhile is chosen as emperor of Rome and married to Leonoreta. Lisuarte thanks Amadís and makes him his heir and recognizes his marriage to Oriana, while Esplandián at last learns who his parents are. They all agree now to go the Ínsola Firme. Amadís rewards his faithful knights. Queen Elisena and Galaor arrive from Gaul and the latter now marries Briolanja. Lisuarte, Queen Brisena, and Leonoreta also come to complete the great gathering.

Urganda now disembarks from a great serpent and presents Esplandián with two youths (one the natural son of Galaor, the other the natural son of King Cildadán and of the nieces of Urganda) to serve him. Nasciano publicly marries Amadís and Oriana, Agrajes and the Norwegian princess Olinda, and Bruneo and Amadís's sister, Melicia. Urganda reviews her past prophecies and how they have come true; she also prophesies Esplandián's future fame and gives Amadís and Oriana magic rings for their protection. Finally, the great festivities over, Amadís and Oriana are left on the Ínsola Firme while all the others return to their domains and kingdoms. [This would seem to be the natural ending of the whole narrative].

Amadís now goes to the help of Darioleta, formerly his mother's damsel, and now wife of the governor of Little Britain, against the giant Balán (descended from contemporaries of King Arthur, Tristan, and Lancelot), who has killed her son and holds her husband and daughter prisoners. Amadís defeats Balán, who now becomes his friend. Amadís, joined by Grasandor, visits another island where he sees a sword driven between two doors and seven white letters and red letters, the white proclaiming that only his son Esplandián can retrieve the sword since he has seven such red letters on his breast and that Urganda has decreed this. On his return Amadís finds Arcaláus's wife, whom he now also locks up. Lisuarte on his way home is captured and taken away by enchantment from Queen Brisena, who sends the news to Amadís and Oriana, and a great search is begun.

Meanwhile Galaor, Balán, Bruneo and many others come to the Ínsola Firme to offer their help. At this Urganda appears again and comforts Oriana and tells the others not to look for the king but to leave it to God. They then dine with Urganda in the great serpent and she gives Esplandián black arms [the sword, as stated, he will win later], and he then keeps vigil before the Virgin's altar, begging her to let him bring back Lisuarte. Next day Urganda orders Balán to knight him. Amadís then asks Esplandián to fulfill his promise to serve the Princess Leonorina, daughter of the emperor of Constantinople, and he gives him her ring. Urganda, the serpent, and Esplandián and his companions then suddenly disappear, but a letter tells Amadís and the others to rest from their deeds of arms and return home, leaving the field for new heroes; Amadís will have to face many upsets and is asked to let God's will be carried out that Esplandián will supersede him; some will say that he killed his father, but this should be taken to mean that his glory will eclipse even that of Amadís. The latter asks them to depart and he sends Galaor and Galvanes to tell Queen Brisena of the position. Amadís, Agrajes, and the others await news on the Ínsola Firme and stand ready to help Lisuarte if this should be necessary.

The Colophon reads: Here end the four books of the brave and very virtuous knight Amadís of Gaul in which are found at length the great adventures and terrible battles which in their times were completed and won by him, and many other knights, his kin as well as his friends. They were printed in the very noble and loyal city of Saragossa by George Coci, German. They were finished on October 30 of the year of the birth of our Savior Jesus Christ 1508.

CHAPTER 3

The Amadís *Question*

THE *Amadís* has been known for at least six-hundred years, and this is again a reminder that we are dealing with a work which has appealed to many generations, both medieval and modern, and that Garci Rodríguez de Montalvo is both transmitter and author. We are in the presence of an ancient product of European literature, which has more than one feature of the anonymity of older things and at the same time can be said to have helped to create the modern novel. For more than half a millennium comments have been made about its author and its country and language of origin. These comments have grown into a tradition known to literary history as "the *Amadís* question," and, since the matter under dispute has not been settled with any finality, the question is still with us. This short chapter will attempt to summarize the subject and to bring up to date the state of *Amadís* studies by referring to what are seen to be the most significant contributions to the field during the past sixty years or so. A full account of the "question" up to 1900 can be found in the important monograph of Miss Grace S. Williams and a critical coverage of the early evidence in the famous essay of Menéndez y Pelayo, both of which will be dealt with below.

References to the *Amadís* date from as early as the mid-1300s, but this fact emerged only during the nineteenth century with the revival of interest in European literature. Before that time the earliest known references, that is, those preceding in time its first known edition of Saragossa, 1508, were confined to the 1400s; the existence of an edition of 1496 is based only on as yet unsubstantiated assertions by early-nineteenth-century specialists. From c. 1344 until 1445 there appeared several references to the novel and to some of its characters. The first of these references is from a Spanish version by García de Castrojeriz of a well-known Latin treatise on politics, by Colonna (Egidius Romanus), while the others

mostly come from poetic texts, namely, the *Rimado de Palacio,*
composed between 1385 and 1400, and the *Cancionero de Baena*
(1445), and two other collections, and they were made by such
literary figures as López de Ayala, Villasandino, Pero Ferrús, and
Juan Alfonso de Baena himself. This precious evidence of its early
fame clearly indicates that our romance existed during the 1300s in a
three-book form at the end of which the hero would appear to have
died, and also shows that he and Oriana were so firmly a part of
courtly culture as to be consistently listed with such figures from the
Breton sources as Lancelot, Guinevere, and Tristan.

In the mid-1400s the chronicler Gomes Eanes de Zurara first
declared that the author of the *Amadís* was a Portuguese, Vasco
Lobeira, from the reign of King Ferdinand (1367–83). This statement was for long seen as a historical document and forms the basis
of the persistent claim by the Portuguese that the *Amadís* is theirs.
In c. 1549 another chronicler, João de Barros, repeated the claim. In
1598 Leitão Ferreira, son of a famous poet, in editing his father's
works, stated that Lobeira lived in the earlier reign of King Denis
(1279–1325) and that the prince involved in suggested changes in
the Briolanja episode (at the end of Book I) was Denis's son; it was
also asserted that the original of the romance was to be found in the
noble house of Aveiro, to the north of Coimbra. The serious dis-
crepany between the dates for Lobeira given by the two chroniclers
became clear only when the Spanish poetic texts were made available, since López de Ayala, who said that he had wasted his youth
listening to the *Amadís* being read, would have done so in the 1340s
at the latest. (Modern attempts have of course been made to reconcile the early references to two Lobeiras.)

Both Spanish and Portuguese and, later, French writers, during
the 1600s and the 1700s, repeated and even elaborated these claims,
and it was also stated that a copy of the romance existed in a noble
house in Vimeiro (near Evora), but that it had been lost; some held
that this took place during the Lisbon earthquake of 1755. The fact
is that no Portuguese manuscript of the *Amadís* has ever been made
available. The Spanish edition of 1508 was followed by some twenty
others before the end of the century and many translations, into
French, German, English, Italian, and Dutch, within the same
period and during the 1600s, as well as by the famous adaptation, in
French, of its nonnarrative material as a handbook of courtly behavior, which was also reprinted, and translated, on many occa-

sions. Thus in the century after its first publication our romance had become a best seller, widely known and quoted throughout Europe. The 1500s also saw many continuations and imitations of the *Amadís* and these too were often translated.

The 1800s witnessed the continuation of the "question," which now became a topic of even more interest in several countries. The English poet Robert Southey translated the romance with comments and this was reviewed by the novelist Sir Walter Scott (both in 1803). A Frenchman, Baret, began in 1853 to cast doubt on the Portuguese case by referring to the early Spanish poetic evidence, although this was challenged from the 1870s by the Portuguese scholars Teófilo Braga and Carolina Michaelis de Vasconcelos, who made much of the discovery in 1880 of the Portuguese original of Princess Leonoreta's little song, attributed to a João Lobeira. The balance of criticism, including that of some German scholars, favored Baret's thesis. The mid-1800s also saw the first modern edition of the *Amadís*, that by Gayangos in 1857, in a famous Spanish series of texts. The early 1900s produced two of the most substantial studies of our romance. First, in 1905 Spain's illustrious scholar Marcelino Menéndez y Pelayo summarized the evidence to date and gave the first true analysis of the novel's contents, its psychology, and its values, while making the claim that it was the first modern novel. Grace Williams, a North American, published in 1909 an even more detailed study which examined in depth the whole question of early references and claims of authorship as well as the history of the "question" up to 1905; she then went on to analyze Montalvo's contributions and changes, and the novel's sources both Breton and other, with some final judgments about its moralistic emphasis and ultimate shape. This monograph cannot be ignored by any student of the *Amadís*.

During the last sixty years or so interest has shifted from authorship and origins to a fresh examination of sources, structure, and meaning. Henry Thomas, in 1920, placed the romance more broadly in its period, while W. J. Entwistle, in 1925, threw much new light on the Breton tradition in the Iberian Peninsula. The Portuguese case has still been argued, sometimes to the point of literary irredentism—chiefly by M. Rodrigues Lapa, over the period 1941–70. While the attribution to Lobeira still stands, and the Briolanja episode still contains a puzzle, Leonoreta's song cannot be used as an argument, since in its Castilian form it could have been inserted at any time. Dr. Rodrigues Lapa says that a Portuguese manuscript exists in Madrid, but this has not been published. Other Portuguese have adopted an attitude more in accordance with the evidence and three abbreviated Portuguese translations have appeared. From Spain in 1947 both Félix Olmedo and Samuel Gili y Gaya drew attention to Montalvo's moralistic and Christian emphasis. In 1948 Dr. Justina Ruiz de Conde produced an important monograph on secret marriage in the Middle Ages, with its application to the *Amadís* (first noticed by Menéndez y Pelayo). P. Bohigas in 1949 and 1951 contributed two very useful essays on the novels of chivalry in the Peninsula and the *Amadís* in particular.

The chief event in *Amadís* studies for a long time was the discovery in 1955 in Spain of four manuscript fragments from the early 1400s: these showed that Nasciano and Esplandián were not creations of Montalvo and that the latter in fact abbreviated rather than elaborated his material, and they were edited and commented on by the three specialists, A. Rodríguez-Moñino, Rafael Lapesa, and A. Millares Carlo (in 1957). In the 1950s and 1960s the North American E. B. Place wrote several articles, of varying quality, on the name "Gaul," on the novel's possible historical background, on its use as a court manual, and on Montalvo's reworking of the older material. Dr. Place is also the author of a critical edition, with abundant accompanying comments and information, of the first known edition of 1508: this came out in four volumes, in 1959–69, and is now the standard text. The late Argentinian scholar María Rosa Lida de Malkiel made two valuable additions to the field, on the primitive form of the romance; she guessed that Esplandián was an early figure. In 1952 and 1959 the same scholar wrote on Peninsular Breton material. Another North American, Anthony Mottola, in a doctoral thesis of 1962, made a comprehensive critical review of the whole *Amadís* field and its problems. In 1967 another Argentinian, Frida Weber de Kurlat, produced the first full-scale study of the novel's structure: this is a detailed analysis of narrative devices, some deriving from historical prose, involving both author and reader and giving the romance its distinctive form of convergence and divergence of movement. Dr. Weber's fundamental study points the way to further much-needed research into the contents of the *Amadís*. Finally, two recent editions, intended for students, have appeared in Barcelona and Mexico City (both in 1969), with useful introductions and bibliographies.

The lengthy history of the "question" has produced a great variety of tributes and studies which have in recent times broadened out into a wider field of true research. Certain areas of the *Amadís*, in particular its language and style and its contents, still remain to be thoroughly analyzed. However, the welcome change in reading tastes since 1900 and the current interest in symbolism and in literary forms bode well for the future. While the traditional preoccupations with origins have not led, and may never lead, to definitive conclusions, there is little doubt that the interest of the *Amadís* for the modern reader is as an outstanding piece of early modern prose fiction which had a quite exceptional influence and fame for over two centuries. Without it we should not have had *Don Quixote* and without Cervantes's masterpiece the modern novel would have been very different. It is hoped in the rest of this monograph to look more closely than others have chosen to do at the contents and the form of the *Amadís*. (Further details of the studies mentioned in this chapter appear in our Selected Bibliography.)

CHAPTER 4

The Structural Features

I *Preliminary Considerations*

M ORE than one reference has already been made to the length and the complexity of our romance. This is, of course, in the nature of the older French prose works from which it derives. Therefore, the question of the structure of the *Amadís* and the way in which it can be shown to derive and differ from that of its models should be considered in some detail and under different aspects at the outset of this further section of our monograph, that is, before the analysis of its contents proper is undertaken. The reader will recall that, at the beginning of Chapter 2 and before a summary of the story and other contents of the *Amadís* was given, some general comment was made on the way the romance is laid out in terms of prologues, chapters, and books, and attention was also drawn to the use of interweaving in the *Amadís*, and to the overall structural pattern of the work. The use of interweaving will be analyzed in some detail below. There will also be attempted an examination of the strictly nonfictional or nonnarrative elements in the romance, that is, the author's reflections, the exhortations and the homilies addressed to certain characters and to humanity at large or the reader, and the significance of these interpolations for the total meaning of the *Amadís* and of the structure itself.

First, and by way of preliminary comment on the material of this chapter, which seeks to examine certain aspects of the *Amadís* in more depth than has been done before, a general word should be said about the literary conventions of Montalvo's age and that of his predecessors. These conventions concerned the relationship of subject and form, and, like those of other periods, they can be brought under the general name of rhetoric. The art of using language persuasively and eloquently was inherited by the Middle Ages from the theory and practice of the ancient world, although new emphases and choices were developed. As far as rhetorical theory bears on the *Amadís*, it can be said to reflect the rules as they apply to long narratives, and its connection with the latter will be referred to more than once below. Rather than a close analysis of the use in our romance of rhetorical practice, a brief account of the latter should suffice, and this should help the reader, in the detailed analyses below, to recognize some of the debts of the *Amadís* to the aesthetic conventions of its time.

In particular, attention should be concentrated on what for the medieval period was seen as the chief function of a writer, namely, the cultivation of *amplificatio*, or the elaboration of the narrative. This mainly took the form of *interpretatio* (the development of the subject), and can, for instance, be illustrated by the inclusion in the *Amadís* of many subsidiary as well as primary episodes, both of which also bring in a large number of characters and places. Other kinds of elaboration were also used, such as periphrasis, comparison, apostrophe, and several forms of digression and description. In addition, all these divisions of the same all-embracing feature of medieval narrative could include direct or indirect references to the physical and moral qualities of the people portrayed; Amadís, for example, is both very handsome and very virtuous, while the Endriago is the epitome of the physically hideous and the morally revolting. Thus our romance, like many of its fellows, uses descriptions to present types worthy of praise or blame or indeed worthy of both, and this attitude to the fictional material is also basic to rhetorical theory. It can therefore be said that much if not all of the *Amadís* is true to the aesthetic standards of its own age. It is, of course, not surprising that this should be so, but it is nevertheless appropriate to make the point clearly, since these standards in certain respects differ from those of our own age. At the same time, passing reference should again be made to the indebtedness of the *Amadís* (and indeed of much early fiction) to the tradition of historical prose, which, of course, in its turn, made use of certain rhetorical features such as apostrophe, comparison, and description.

Second, the reader will recall the reference in Chapter 3 to the only truly detailed study of the structure of our romance, the masterly essay of Dr. Frida Weber. This concerns itself with an analysis of the several kinds of narrative formulae employed throughout, and mostly designed to orientate the reader among the romance's many paths and incidents; the author at times even uses his reader's supposed fatigue as an excuse for not lengthening his story. The most common formula—and it is a very common one indeed—employs the verb *oír* (to hear), for instance in phrases such as: "como oýs" ("as you hear"), "como oýstes" ("as you heard"), "como oyréys" ("as you will hear"), or "como auedes oýdo" ("as you have heard"). These devices look both backward and forward in the narrative. Some of the formulae tend to turn the author himself into a character in his own book, and thus form what Dr. Weber calls an "internal link" within the story, while others (forming an "external link") involve the reader and the author together. These latter are more common in the *Amadís*, although both types recall practice in Spanish historical prose, from the chronicles of Alfonso X onward. The devices are used to organize a long narrative, and they thus provide variety, keep the attention alive, and generally give recognizable shape to the abundant material. Dr. Weber also shows that both kinds of device are more systematically used in Books III and IV than in the first part of the work, and this is particularly the case with those of the prospective and the retrospective kinds. This concentration of features in Books III and IV plus the general references throughout to specific books or parts (this latter a device not to be found in the chronicles) would seem to strengthen the thesis that Montalvo reworked and added to the older material to produce his own *Amadís*, and that the later part of the work appears to bear more traces of his remolding hand.

Dr. Weber also refers to all these devices as typical of the early or primitive European novel, chiefly because they almost always result in a lack of the surprise element, itself rather more typical of much fiction of later periods—indeed, dramatic suspense occurs very seldom and in few if any of the major episodes of the *Amadís*. It may be worth commenting here that not all early fiction was lacking in surprise, since interweaving itself was partly designed to terminate an action with little warning. Still, it is to be noted that not all generations of readers looked for the same things and effects in their enjoyment of fiction. On the other hand, it could be said—as in fact it has been suggested in our Chapter 1 and as Dr. Weber well demonstrates—that the *Amadís*, as it has come down to us, has a general structural similarity to works written according to those prescriptions more typical of postmedieval literature when the older European rules of rhetoric were to be set aside in favor of the resurrected precepts of antiquity. This is to say that our romance develops toward clearly perceptible climaxes and ends on a triumphant note, even if at the very end the door is kept open for further adventures of Amadís and of his son and successor.

Be this as it may—and we shall later look again at the overall structure—it could also be added to Dr. Weber's revealing examination of the *Amadís* that our romance provides a very striking example of what Wayne Booth calls "the rhetoric of fiction" (in his famous monograph of the same name): the constant intervention or "voice" of the author and his equally constant, if one-sided, address to the reader both constitute a clear case of authorial control and of interpreted reality, together, in this case, as we shall see, with very explicit statements of values meant to guide the reader's understanding of the story. Dr. Booth does not use the *Amadís* to illustrate his ideas, but he does exemplify some of his theses from the practice of our romance's most famous successor, *Don Quixote.*

II *Interweaving and Other Features*

Any attentive reader will soon perceive that the *Amadís,* with its many facets and its great variety of subject material, is an articulated artistic unity, as, indeed, Dr. Weber stresses in her conclusions. The following more detailed treatment of the work will attempt to present it from different points of view and under several headings, and thus some overlapping will inevitably occur in the process. Also, the romance will be traversed on more than one occasion, and in following these analyses the reader is aked to refer to the summary of the story given in Chapter 2.

It will be recalled that mention has been made of the Arthurian romances and of their impact in the Iberian Peninsula (see Chapter 1). It is also part of the accumulated and accepted truth about the *Amadís* that its chief source is the famous French prose romance *Li Livres de Lancelot (The Book of Lancelot).* This romance has survived in about a hundred manuscripts and also ran into seven printed editions in the period 1488–1533. This French *Lancelot* is the version belonging to the so-called Vulgate cycle of prose romances, composed in all probability within the period 1215–25; it superseded and expanded the earlier verse narratives of Chrétien de Troyes, from the late 1100s. The slightly later thirteenth-century version of the Tristan story (which is also mentioned in the *Amadís;* see Chapter 2) was influenced in its turn by the Vulgate romances.

The actual version of the *Lancelot* used by the first composer of the *Amadís* is unknown, but fragments of the French romance in Portuguese-Galician, Catalan, and Castilian survive from the late 1300s and the early 1400s, although these derive from the so-called Post-Vulgate cycle, once supposed to be the work of a Robert de Boron, from the period 1230–40, and not from the Vulgate cycle as such.

The similarities between the *Amadís* and the older romances, chiefly the *Lancelot* and the *Tristan,* are to be found throughout the Spanish work and many of them are fundamental. Thus the main characters, and their appellations as well as their relationships— their loves, their jealousies, and their mortal hatreds—all have parallels in the French models. This is also true, for instance, of the Ínsola Firme and Amadís's travels in Europe, not to mention the great battles with the emperor of Rome or the fearful encounter with the Endriago, and many other single episodes. The *Gran Conquista de Ultramar* also provides several parallels with the *Amadís* (modern scholarship has suggested that the non-Arthurian sources of the *Amadís* still form a subject of fruitful research). Esplandián (a name of Trojan origin) would appear to have been a truly new creation of the Spanish romance, and we also now know that this character was not invented by Montalvo. All in all, the *Amadís* must in justice be regarded as essentially neo-Arthurian, but equally it is a most original remaking and development of this material of common European stock.[1]

Returning to the subject of the preliminary part of this chapter, some account will now be given of the structural features inherited by the author of the *Amadís,* and of their modification. Several of the romances of the Vulgate cycle, including the *Lancelot,* make use of the device of interweaving or, in French, *entrelacement,* a term first applied to the phenomenon by the scholar Fernand Lot in 1918. The feature consists of interrupting one narrative episode by introducing another, and in turn the interruption of the latter in order to take up the earlier one, and so on with other new episodes or stories. The effect of this device is to knit together several narrative strands and to keep more than one tale alive at the same time. It is clearly a method of enlarging the subject matter, in the general tradition of *amplificatio,* while preserving a kind of coherence. The resultant "maze of adventures," as it has been called, say in the

Lancelot, has in the past perplexed several eminent medievalists, who proceeded to condemn the practice and to regard the narrative pattern thus produced as lacking in recognized form.

Recent reconsideration of the whole question, however, has produced a defense of such a structure on the grounds that the medieval aesthetic view of artistic unity differs genuinely and radically from the modern one. The latter more closely echoes the Aristotelian view that a composition has its clear beginning, middle, and end, and can thus be easily envisaged; it also subordinates one element to another and rigorously selects the components. On the other hand, the medieval world seemed to give great preference to elaboration of different kinds, and reference has already been made to the importance of this practice for the rhetoricians of the age. Where we tend to aim at unity through simplicity, our ancestors went for expansion through growth and diversity of elements. Interweaving has also been called "interlace," and can be shown to have its parallels in the medieval plastic arts. Thus the mind trained to look for clear narrative progression will easily get lost in trying to follow a theme or character that disappears and then reappears much later. This older and now long abandoned form of storytelling demands for its enjoyment a special ability. One who has made a detailed study of the subject puts it thus: "The fascination of tracing a theme through all its phases, of waiting for its return while following other themes, of experiencing the constant sense of their simultaneous presence, depends upon our grasp of the entire structure—the most elusive that has ever been devised." (See E. Vinaver, *The Rise of Romance,* Oxford, 1971, p. 81.)

This method of narration also provides its own form of continuity, of unfolding variety, and of final completeness, all of which finds echoes both in the characterization and in the episodes. Further, it held the attention of many generations of readers and listeners, from the tenth-century Old English epic of *Beowulf* to the 1500s. Thus it was still used by Ariosto in his *Orlando furioso* (published in its final form in 1532), and this gave rise to one of the major literary controversies of the age between his admirers and those of Torquato Tasso. Cervantes, as is well known, parodied it in his *Don Quixote,* although the latter's structure developed much beyond the older conventions and thus anticipated and suggested the form of the modern novel.

The *Amadís* partakes of this hallowed canon, although it is hoped that its use will not act as an obstacle to the modern reader who is accustomed to a different tradition of imaginative order. (It has already been stated that our romance also displays adherence to the newer rules of composition.) All long narrations make special demands on the rules of structure and shape, and thus their study should pay close attention to the divisions of the material employed for their telling.

Although Dr. Weber did not mention interweaving, it is in fact implicit in her analysis. Let us see how this very important device is employed in the *Amadís*.

Book I introduces interweaving early on, when in Chapter 2 (that is, the third chapter division, if one recalls that the first one is unnumbered) the narrative leaves King Perión and returns to Gandales, who was then rearing the infant Amadís. Up to this point the story had proceeded without interruption. Thus we are told how Amadís's parents, Perión and Elisena, met in Little Britain, how he was born and abandoned after his father's departure, and how the latter had his dream interpreted. Then the author returns with little delay to his hero and he keeps with him to tell us of Urganda's first appearance and prophecy concerning his great future, and (in Chapter 3) of his adoption by King Languines, Gandales's master. In the same Chapter 3 the narrative is again interrupted as we return to Perión and Elisena and their marriage and the birth and early kidnapping of Galaor, Amadís's brother and later very loyal companion. We also now get a very brief account of Lisuarte's assumption of power as king of Great Britain and a first mention of his daughter, Oriana.

Thus in a short space several of the main characters are introduced to the reader by means of interweaving. Chapter 4 opens with a return to the now youthful Amadís, his first meeting with Oriana, and his love for her and his knighting by Perión. Here Urganda appears for a second time and gives Amadís a lance with which he wins his first battle by rescuing Perión, while at the same time he shows the first intense effects of his passion for Oriana. After a very short return to Galaor and his early training in arms, we are given (in Chapters 6 and 7) a longer unbroken account of the successive adventures and acts of prowess of Amadís. In Chapter 8 Oriana is brought back from Scotland to her father Lisuarte's court and she sends Amadís a letter telling how she knows of his secret origin. The further adventures of the war in Gaul against Abiés of

Ireland and Amadís's and his cousin Agrajes's part in them now
follow, with victory for Perión and his recognition of Amadís as his
son (Chapters 8–10). This further longer narrative (unbroken but for
the brief interludes of Agrajes and the Damsel of Denmark) now
links directly with Amadís's knighting of his brother Galaor at
Urganda's instigation, and with Galaor's own adventures as he too
goes to Lisuarte's court (Chapters 11–12). The further adventures of
Amadís bring him to the court and Oriana, while Galaor's and
Agrajes's adventures continue (Chapters 13–17), thus setting up a
kind of steady rhythm of interweaving, which, however, goes together with what Dr. Weber calls convergent and divergent
movements toward and away from Lisuarte's court at Vindilisora
(Windsor), and in which the alternatives of action again succeed
each other at a more developed length.

This pattern now continues with the enchantment by Arcaláus of
Amadís and further acts of heroism by Galaor, Baláys, and Amadís
himself, who for the moment is away from the court (and this takes
us up to Chapter 28). Chapter 26 includes a meeting between
Amadís and the knight who took Galaor's horse, and our hero's
defeat of him provides one of several examples of how this burgeoning material can have its loose ends tied up from time to time.
At this point Amadís and Galaor consider that a round of adventures
has been honorably concluded and they go together to the *cortes,* or
assembly, called by Lisuarte for London (Chapter 29), which clearly
forms a first culmination or climax in the development of the
Amadís. This assembling of many knights also allows them to renew
vows to protect ladies and damsels and thus underline their motives
in setting out on fresh adventures. The solemn marriage of Angriote
and his lady also emphasizes the values being discussed (thus we
reach Chapter 31).

The rest of Book I, still making some use of interweaving in
relating Galaor's and Amadís's further new adventures, is first taken
up with the enchantment of Lisuarte and his court by Arcaláus and
the eventual liberation of Oriana by Amadís, with the freeing of
Lisuarte by Galaor, the overthrow of the usurper Barsinán, and then
the holding of the new and greater assembly in London (this takes us
up to Chapter 39). At this point new material and characters are
brought in to provide further adventures for Amadís and his followers: it is now that Amadís fulfills his vow to help Queen Briolanja
(made to her as a "niña fermosa," or beautiful child or girl, as far

back as Chapter 21). This outcome exemplifies a certain feature of interweaving, namely, delayed recognition or identification, of which there are a good few throughout the *Amadís*. Here too our author gives the conflicting accounts of how Briolanja fell in love with Amadís and tried to seduce him (this part of the whole episode, it will be recalled, was to become one of the recurring items in the "*Amadís* question"). In Chapter 41 we are introduced to Florestán, Amadís and Galaor's half brother, who, knighted by Galaor, is also to become a most loyal follower of Amadís. Briolanja lavishly rewards Amadís and his companions for their defeat of Abíseos, but also causes mortal jealousy in Oriana.

It will be seen that this last section of Book I makes much less use of interweaving but rather tends to let episodes develop and thus slows down the rhythm of change of scene characteristic of this narrative method. We also find here too that the number of different episodes is correspondingly reduced. While it is true that Amadís and Galaor in particular have many encounters and adventures both before and after the first and second London assembly, it will also have been noted that the multiplying incidents are, as stated above, arranged and made to serve the meetings at Lisuarte's court.

Having looked at Book I for evidence of interweaving in its developing structure—it is in fact used some twenty times—we see that this device is modified as the narrative proceeds toward its point of climax, namely, the *cortes* in London (the text states that the city "a la sazón como vna águila encima de lo más de la cristiandad estaua"; that is, "it stood then like an eagle over most of Christendom"). Here too Lisuarte is identified as the true leader of all virtuous knights; he is of course also the father of Oriana, with whom Amadís now consummates his love and makes lasting vows. It is at this assembly of rededication to chivalry that Amadís recalls his vow to Briolanja and thus originates the final set of episodes in Book I.

This book also uses, sparingly, the prospective and retrospective devices which are, however, to appear increasingly in the later books. Thus in Chapter 19 Amadís's vow to the wife of Arcaláus, we are told, will be fulfilled in Book IV, while Arcaláus's further deeds at this point are also postponed. Other examples of the same device occur in Chapters 21 and 30, while the device of omission occurs once together with yet another case of prospection (in Chapter 42). The practice of reminding the reader of past events will occur more

naturally in the later books as the narrative pattern expands even
further. In any case, the already very significant developments in
Book I, which take us from the birth of Amadís to his acceptance as
the greatest of knights, not only set the scene but prepare the way
for much that is to follow. Further, Book I also demonstrates how
motivation, based on social and other values and on emotional attachments, can dictate the course of action and events. The so-called
psychological and ideological elements in our romance constitute a
significant part of its totality and they also respond to its rhetorical
structure. These elements will be examined more closely below.

What of interweaving and some of the other emerging structural
features in Books II–IV? It will be recalled that Book II is chiefly
concerned with the Ínsola Firme and with Amadís's final possession
of it, with his departure to the Peña Pobre, and the events leading
up to his departure from Lisuarte's court. This is set out in longer
chapters, and, like Book III, Book II has fewer chapters than Books
I or IV. Also, only three clear cases of interweaving occur (in
Chapters 42, 55, and 64), and they are clearly spaced out at the
beginning, in the middle, and at the end. There are, however, two
cases of alternative but related devices: one (in Chapter 48) in which
the story is brought up to date by leaving the current episode (that
dealing with Amadís as the hermit Beltenebrós) and going back; the
other (Chapter 63) in which two narrative strands are tied together
(that is, by the telling to Oriana of Briolanja's adventures in the
Ínsola Firme). These, of course, are familiar devices to be found in
all kinds of fiction.

In addition, Book II uses other devices, some of them already
noted in Book I, which are to become very common in Books III and
IV. Thus the denial or refusal by the author to take the story
further—sometimes, as noted, with the excuse that it may weary the
reader—although this device can merely concern sallies that come
to nothing, in Chapters 48, 53, and 56. This is in fact a device that
produces the opposite result from that of interweaving. Again, a
prospective device to be much used later, namely, anticipation or
the sending of the reader to a later point in the narrative, occurs
several times (Chapters 48, 49, 54, 59, and 62). Again, we have two
examples (Chapters 44 and 53 and more frequently later) of the
retrospective device of reminding the reader of past events. It will
be seen that Book II prefigures the general structural pattern of the
remaining two books, that is, as the narrative concentrates more and

more upon certain characters and the results of their intentions and actions, chiefly the love of Amadís and Oriana and the stubborn pride of Lisuarte.

Book III covers Esplandián's birth, Amadís's journeying in central and eastern Europe, the arranged marriage for Oriana with El Patín, and her liberation by Amadís from Salustanquidio's fleet. This book thus further illustrates the two chief psychological springs of action which in fact now come into conflict with each other. Interweaving has been noted only once in Book III (in Chapter 66), although it is rather an example of taking up a related thread of the story. On the other hand, the other devices noted in Book II occur in some abundance. The device of anticipation sends the reader forward no fewer than twelve times, including several specific references to what will happen in Book IV. Of these, two (in Chapter 74) mention by name the *Sergas de Esplandián*, the continuation of the *Amadís* in which the deeds of our hero's son and successor will be told. Once more the deliberate avoidance or denial of further detail is used, six times in all: at the very beginning, in the unnumbered chapter, it serves the purpose of anticipation as well as avoiding prolixity, while in another case the story is cut short specifically because it does not bear directly on Amadís as our chief hero. Thus once again we meet with the very opposite of interweaving, that is, a device which belongs to the unifying method of narration. In addition, Book III has five cases where the reader is reminded of what has happened: important examples of this are when King Trafinor of Bohemia recalls to Amadís his earlier deeds, but as the Knight of the Green Sword the latter denies knowledge of such a man or his deeds (in Chapter 70), and when we are told again (in Chapter 72) of the background to El Patín's passion for Oriana, that is, when its consequences are about to develop. Finally, we meet early in this book with three cases of characters within the story being brought up to date with events, and one rare case, also at the beginning, of characters disappearing from the narrative for good (the evildoers Gandandel and Brocadán after their defeat and their sons' death). It would seem that those who believe that Montalvo took material from Book III and changed what was left can find some support from the kind and frequency of the structural devices employed.

Book IV, introduced by Montalvo as his "discovery," is from the first seen as presenting the life of the Christian knight; it also contains a good many references to Esplandián as his father's successor. In fact, it deals largely with the consequences of Lisuarte's pride, already very evident in Book III. Thus, with the return of Amadís from Constantinople, large armies are collected on both sides, with help from as far away as Rome and Ireland, while Arcaláus gets ready to take advantage of both forces. The destructive conflict is ended by the holy man Nasciano, and, after the near defeat of Lisuarte by Arcaláus and his companions, the former makes peace with our hero and many marriages and settlements follow. This, the obvious final climax, it would appear, is, however, itself followed by Amadís's further adventures with Balán and Darioleta. The reappearance of the latter, in Chapter 147, constitutes another striking structural throwback, to the first chapters of the *Amadís* when she was Queen Elisena's lady attendant. This reappearance as indicated before is also a feature of interweaving, and an earlier example, in Chapter 69, concerns the lady whom Amadís frees from Arcaláus and who tells him it was she who cast him as a baby into the sea. There is also the last revelation concerning Esplandián, and the spiriting away of Lisuarte, whose freeing is to be left to Esplandián, now knighted and carried off by Urganda.

Book IV is the longest of the four in pages and chapters, and this concentration of subject matter would also seem to explain the exceptional use in it of the structural devices we have been examining above. Thus, as against Books II and III, interweaving is used no fewer than ten times, while anticipation or prophecy occurs in all fifteen times; naturally, some of these refer explicitly to Esplandián and his future deeds in the *Sergas*. The device of omission, or cutting short the narrative, is likewise employed several times (in all some nine times, with, in Chapters 105 and 109, special rhetorical use being made of the impossibility of telling all about the preparations for the great battle between Lisuarte and Amadís). Interestingly, however, but, again understandably, given the extent of the material and perhaps also the very great probability that Montalvo recast the work, the device of reminding the reader or recapitulation by one character to another is easily the most used, even exceeding the appearance of interweaving in Book I, with a total of no fewer than twenty-six examples. (A striking case in Chapter 97 allows Amadís's adventures in eastern Europe to be told by Grasinda to Oriana and the other ladies in the Ínsola Firme.) Dr. Frida Weber had stressed that this device, except when it refers the reader to precise places in the narrative, recalls clearly the dependence of the *Amadís* on Spanish historical prose. There are a few main threads running through Book IV, which, like its immediate predecessor, is dominated by the great battles and their dire results. Nevertheless, there still occurs a variety of adventures recalling the earlier parts of the romance, and it is to cope with this multiplying of material, as we have seen, that interweaving is required.

To sum up: the *Amadís* still bears clear structural traces of the pattern inherited from the Vulgate prose romances. Thus interweaving is a clearly discernible feature of Book I, although even here there are a few early examples of the competing devices of anticipation or postponement and deliberate omission or curtailment. There is, of course, also in Book I the clear narrative progression toward the meeting at Lisuarte's court. Book II makes much less use of interweaving, thus concentrating the story on Amadís and using other devices, whereas in Book III we get an almost total disappearance of interweaving, but an equally remarkable increase in anticipation. It is, of course, the case that the action of Book III is divided between different areas of action. If it is true that at this point in the narrative Montalvo reduced the material of Books II and III and made other changes in order to expand the work into Book IV, then the above examples of the narrative pattern would seem to give force to the contention. We have seen how Dr. Weber's researches have led her to a similar conclusion and we also note the comments of Dr. Mottola. Also in Book IV there is an increased use of the devices binding that narrative strands together and thus creating a more explicit unity. Interweaving reappears quite frequently and thus recalls the earlier narrative pattern. The overall picture of Book IV, however, is of the progression toward the climax of battles, thus echoing the convergence toward the court in Book I.[2]

Finally, it is worth noting that several of the narrative devices analyzed by Dr. Weber as well as the one examined here for the first time in the *Amadís*, namely, interweaving, are also employed in the two contemporary Spanish editions of the romances, *Tristán de Leonís* (1501) and *La demanda del Sancto Grial* (1515). They are also to be seen in the *Sergas de Esplandián* (or Book V of the *Amadís*), of 1510, which in addition has some of the authorial interventions to be looked at below.

By approaching the *Amadís* through its anatomical frame, as it were, it is hoped to suggest both its variety and its progression. The story at the very end does not, as we know, terminate, since its continuation is clearly anticipated. Nevertheless, the four-book *Amadís* does possess a beginning, a middle, and an end of its own, with the rise, the setbacks, the trials, and the triumphs of Amadís, and his eventual coming to power as the heir and son-in-law of King Lisuarte.

III   *Authorial Comments*

Another way of uncovering the structure and meaning of the *Amadís* is through an examination of its strictly nonnarrative and nondescriptive material to which more than one reference has already been made and which has been variously named. This chiefly takes the form of a recurrent intervention or reflection of the author, in the shape of moralistic comments, both of commendation and condemnation, and these are often expressed as the rhetorical feature of apostrophe. Professor Vinaver has stated that such "explanatory observations and discourses" belong to the later, more modern narrative conventions and are alien to the practice of interweaving, which rather seeks "amplification and expansion of the matter itself" for its coherence.[3] It is also true, as Dr. Weber has made clear, that the role of the author in the *Amadís* recalls rather the primitive novel, but it must at the same time be stated that the use of this material (employed, as we shall see, like other features already noted, increasingly in the latter part of the romance) again gives a shape and a progression not characteristic of its models. Further, these narrative pauses or interruptions of another kind reveal the ideological core of the work, although, as stated above, such values must be taken together with the psychological motives of the characters themselves.

We cannot, of course, be certain that Montalvo was responsible for all the intercalated passages of comment, although, as we have seen, he states in his prologue that he has added "exemplos y doctrinas" ("examples and teaching") to the emended text of the romance. However this may be, in Chapter 13 we come across the first case of authorial intervention when, just after the inconclusive encounter of Amadís with the proud knight Dardán, the narrative is interrupted thus (this and subsequent quotations have been translated by the author from E. B. Place's edition of the *Amadís*, of which the relevant volume and page numbers are given in each case):

Here the author gives a picture of the proud and speaks thus: O proud men, what do you want, and what is your intention? I beg you to tell me whether your beautiful person, your great valor, the courage of your heart, have by chance been inherited by you from your parents, whether you purchased them with riches, whether you acquired it in the schools of the great scholars, or whether you won it through the favor of great princes. Certainly you will say no. Then, where did you get them? It seems to me that you got them from that very exalted Lord from whom all good things occur and come. And to this Lord what thanks or services do you give in payment for this? Surely none other but to scorn the virtuous and dishonor the good. (I, 109)

This address to all the proud, including presumably some readers, then cites the ancient cases of Lucifer, Nimrod the Hunter and builder of Babel, and Laomedon, king of Troy, all of whom were overthrown because of their pride.

The two sections of this little homily are constructed on those figures of speech typical of sermons, such as rhetorical questions, anaphora, and other forms of repetition. There is perhaps a special significance in that this first "example" should concern itself with the worst of all sins and the one that will also later cause such important figures as King Lisuarte or the Roman emperor El Patín to bring great destruction and distress on themselves and on many others. We might indeed see here suggested much of what is to follow. The author in fact ends his peroration thus: "the history will show it to you later"—that is, that the proud will be shown by events how badly they will fare. Finally, it is worth pointing out that the act of pride which gave rise to this short sermon was done against Amadís, who is already emerging as the champion of the weak and as the paragon of virtues. Pride can, of course, be seen to have certain positive aspects, and thus all knightly exploits can be said to illustrate, one way or another, the concept of "soberbia" (or, in Latin, "superbia"). Indeed, the English word "superb" still recalls the original meaning of the concept.

Just before the next deliberate pause for reflection by the author, and the meeting of the great London assembly, there occurs a brief warning statement (at the beginning of Chapter 31), which runs as follows and whose import for what is to follow (in the rest of the romance) is very clear:

Just as God in his mercy made this king Lisuarte as a disinherited prince, and through the death of his brother King Falangrís, king of Great Britain, in the same way He, since all things are permitted and guided by Him, caused so many knights, so many princesses, daughters of kings and many others from foreign lands, of great style and high lineage, to come to serve Lisuarte with great affection, so that none of them was satisfied if he couldn't call himself the king's man. And since such affairs because of our weak nature bring pride and with pride even great lack of gratitude and recognition of that Lord who grants these things, fortune was allowed by Him, by placing certain difficult obstacles before him, to darken that bright glory in which he resided, to soften his heart and place it in every kind of flabbiness, so that, as he followed rather the service of the giver of all mercies than the tainted appetite which they produce, Lisuarte might be upheld in that great state and might himself become even greater and, acting to the contrary, he should still be tormented with a greater and more perilous fall. (I, 250)

Ominously the author ends this reflection on the fall of a prince with these words: "it was there [i.e., London] that there overcame him the first stratagems of fortune which placed his person and kingdoms in danger of being sundered in two, as will now be told to you" (I, 251).

   This and other such passages in the original are written in clumsy, Latinized syntax typical of the discursive European prose of the time, with its lengthy sentences and its gerundive clauses, which lead to a certain ambiguity for the modern reader. Certain paraphrasing has been necessary in translating these extracts. At the end of this same chapter the author comments briefly on the personal bravery and on the moral continence of Angriote in winning his bride Grovenesa. This is the first of the comments in praise of personal virtues.

   The next full authorial interruption occurs in Chapter 35 and again concerns the same public matter of the fall, if temporary, of a prince, namely, King Lisuarte, who, with his daughter Oriana and others, has been taken prisoner by Arcaláus. This address, directed to the mighty of the world, also deserves to be quoted here, both because it reveals the explicit Christian viewpoint of the author in handling his story, and because it serves as an indirect pointer to Lisuarte's future:

What shall we say here, oh emperors, kings and mighty ones who are placed in high estate? This king Lisuarte on one day thought he was lord of the world with his greatness, and on the same day having lost his daughter and the heiress of his kingdoms, and having been himself taken prisoner, dishonored and in chains, found himself in the power of an evil enchanter and without remedy. Be careful, be careful, and hold to your knowledge of God, for, although He gives great and high estates, He wishes our wills and hearts to be humble and lowly, not regarded so highly that the thanks and services which He deserves may be forgotten, since that with which you wish to uphold your positions, namely, great pride, excessive covetousness, and which is the opposite of what He wishes. He will bring to nought for you with equal dishonor. And above all think of His secret and great judgments, for, if He allowed such a cruel reverse to come to such a just, generous, and gracious king as this Lisuarte, what will He do to those who are in everything his opposite? (I, 278)

At the beginning of Chapter 39, too, just after the second assembly in London, which follows Lisuarte's liberation, the author again returns to the same theme, which it is clearly his intention to underline more and more as his tale unfolds:

Well, just as you hear, King Lisuarte was in London with such knights, and his fame ran higher than that of any prince there had ever been in the world. Fortune was for a long period of time content not to tempt him further, since it had placed him in the great peril of which you have heard, believing it to be sufficient for such a wise and honorable man as he was. It could, however, change if the king should change his purpose through covetousness, through pride and the many other things with which kings, because they are not willing to guard themselves against them, are harmed and their reputations darkened, with even more dishonor and debasement than if the great things that have taken place for their benefit and great glory had not come to them; no one should count himself unfortunate unless he has had good fortune, and this is so only with those who, having achieved these to the height of heaven itself, have then through their bad judgment, their vices and sins attracted fortune to themselves so that it has with pain and anguish taken these things from them.(I, 304–305)

The last two authorial comments proper in Book I are of the same order and form. First we have a kind of extended gloss (in Chapter 42) on the happy outcome of the defeat of the tyrannical usurper Abíseos and the restoration to Briolanja of her kingdom by Amadís and his knights. This comment, called a "Consiliaria," or a set of admonitions, is couched in the same language of sermonizing with

direct address to all concerned, in this case the covetous like
Abíseos who abuse power and ignore God's commandments:

Take example, covetous men, those to whom great lordships are given by
God to govern, and who are not only forgetful of giving thanks to Him for
having placed you in such an exalted position, but, acting against His
commandments, and having lost the fear due to Him, are not content with
those estates which He gave you, and which came to you from your ancestors; rather, with killings, fires, and acts of stealing, you are ready to
usurp the estates of others who live in the law of truth. In this way you flee
and depart from any intention of turning your rages and covetousnesses
against the infidels, in which it would all be well employed, and thus you do
not wish to enjoy that great glory which our Catholic Monarchs enjoy and
will enjoy in this world and the next, since they undertook this by serving
God with many labors. (I, 342)

Montalvo here gives his discourse a contemporary note with the
reference to Ferdinand and Isabella, already singled out, it will be
recalled, in his Prologue. The humble folk are also addressed in
their role as advisers to the great:

And you the lesser people, for those to whom fortune has given so much
power and place, placed as you are in their councils to guide them, just as
the rudder guides and steers the great ship, counsel them faithfully, love
them, since in them you serve God, you serve the generality of people. And
although you do not achieve the satisfaction of your desires from this world,
you will achieve it from the next world, which is without end. (I, 342)

After further consideration of the role of the good counselor, the
author rounds off his homily by returning to the specific case in hand
and its fearful outcome:

. . . the Lord of the world, who puts up with many insults and is a com-
passionate pardoner of them, that is, after all due knowledge and repentence, and there being here no cruel revenger, then allowed to come there
that harsh executioner Amadís of Gaul, who by killing Abíseos and his sons,
thus avenged that great treachery which had been done to that noble king;
. . . do not believe that in this Abíseos paid for and purged his fault; on the
contrary, the souls which with little knowledge of Him who created them,
for their errors and the sins in which they have shared, will be damned
eternally without repair in cruel hell and in burning flames. (I, 343–344)

Finally, and as the very last paragraph of Book I, our author answers his own rhetorical question on power and riches, and in doing so leaves the reader on a note of affirmation and optimism, after the severe reflections expressed on several occasions:

Well, let us now consider these great estates and these riches which bring us such anguish, trouble, pains, and worries to win them, and, once won, to keep them up. Would it be better to give them up and despise them as superfluous and cruel tormentors of our bodies and even more of our souls, seeing that they are neither certain nor lasting? I would certainly say so. Rather I would affirm that, since they have been won in good truth . . . and if we give satisfaction for them to that Lord who provides them, . . . we will be able in this world to achieve rest, pleasure and glory, and in the next everlasting world . . . enjoy in glory the fruit of them. (I, 353–354)

Thus by the end of his first book our author has asked us no fewer than five times to think about the meaning of what we have been reading. This is to be done in terms of man's propensity to evildoing and of God's will for him. These comments, which occur chiefly in the last few chapters, concern both Amadís as the champion of good causes and also King Lisuarte as the beneficiary and victim of his own power. Both these figures will dominate the rest of the novel, the first increasingly as the prototype of chivalry, the second as a great man who, however, becomes corrupted (as we know, Lisuarte's actions are to determine Amadís's own decisions and to cause the series of crises right up to the end of the romance). The other main area of action, namely, the love affair of Amadís and Oriana, is, of course, connected with his relationships with her father, but it is to receive later and separate treatment. A brief comment on the harsh effects of Oriana's jealousy, which is to separate her from Amadís, had been made at the beginning of Chapter 40, but this serves to introduce action rather than to interpret it as a true comment.

Mention should also be made here of what is perhaps the most famous and the most discussed comment by the author of the *Amadís*, namely, that concerning the different versions of the episode of Amadís's relations with Queen Briolanja and of the intervention of a Prince Alfonso of Portugal in the matter. This, however, concerns the story itself rather than its meaning or import, although it is also true that the version preferred by the author

(Montalvo is certainly involved since there is here too a reference to Book IV of the romance) maintains unblemished Amadís's love for Oriana and thus his moral standing as a faithful knight and hero of the whole novel.

These intercalated comments, as has been stated above, continue and indeed increase in number. There are some six such interruptions of the story in Book II, but nine in Book III and eleven in Book IV. First, commenting on Amadís's possession of the Ínsola Firme, his retreat and the symbol of his virtuous life, the author (at the beginning of Book II in Chapter 44) states how even Amadís, with all his steadfastness and bravery, will succumb to events and how only God will see him through to eventual happiness. Soon afterward (in Chapter 48), when Amadís is already in the distant Peña Pobre as a hermit and a self-exile, afflicted by Oriana's jealousy, and forgetful of his duties as a knight, the author comments on his foolishness as a lover, a fresh topic for such moralizing, but one often used as a counter to the prevalent cult of courtly love of Montalvo's age. In a series of rhetorical questions we are told that only God and Amadís's own deeds saved him. This is an important example of authorial admonition since it brings together Amadís's involvement in the main action of the romance as a champion and his role as a lover, overcome by "la yra y la saña de vna flaca mujer" ("the anger and the rage of a weak woman"), even as Hercules, Samson, Solomon, and Aeneas themselves were victims of the same passion. In this Book II, so much concerned with Amadís and Oriana, there is yet another (rather indirect) reference to God's mercy in rescuing Amadís from his despair (Chapter 56).

Later (in Chapter 62) we reach a clear watershed in events. Recalling his earlier comments in Book I, the author asks the reader to consider the great good fortune of Lisuarte, risen by chance to be king of Great Britain, and with a court to which all good and great men come, and how this is to be undone "con causa tan liuiana" ("for such slight cause"), once, in a memorable phrase, God allows man free choice: "afloxadas las riendas, alçada la mano, apartando su gracia" ("the reins being loosened, the hand lifted, and taking away His grace"). We are now close to Lisuarte's fateful deception by Brocadán and Gandandel, and all that flows from his acceding to their evil designs. This certainly constitutes a very important crisis in the *Amadís*, with the breakup of the world of chivalry so firmly portrayed in Book I, and with the revelation of another side of the character of the formerly acknowledged head of the institution, Lisuarte.

Immediately afterward (still in Chapter 62), the author again addresses "reyes y grandes señores que el mundo gouernáys" ("kings and great lords who govern the world"), and tells them how important it is to choose good advisers (this is an ironic gloss on the similar admonition in Chapter 42, commented upon above). As if this were not comment enough, later again in the same chapter we have the author's thoughts on Lisuarte's rejection of Amadís's request on behalf of Galvanes and Madasima, which brings Book II to its climax. This is a distinctly rhetorical outburst made up of two exclamatory statements lamenting the way Lisuarte has ignored Amadís's services and has listened to an evil man. Then there is a reiteration of the theme of lords and their advisers: "Thus, great lords, to whom in this world so much power is given, which suffices to fulfill your appetite and satisfy your wills, guard yourselves from the evil; for since they take little care of themselves and their souls, much less and with more reason must one believe they will have care for your souls" (II, 548).

The important decision of Oriana regarding Esplandián also occurs before the end of Book II, thus reminding us that the author's interpretation of this book has kept before us both the deepening love affair of Amadís and Oriana and the deteriorating moral position of Lisuarte. That is, when halfway through Montalvo's four-book romance, we are fully aware of the likely development of the other half, even if not in any precise detail.

In the unnumbered opening chapter of Book III passing reference is made to Lisuarte's generous and kind reception of Amadís's messengers, thus demonstrating the superiority of loyalty won through such acts over riches, and this makes the author recall the case of the unsubornable Roman senator Fabricius who remained faithful to his commission and refused all blandishments. Shortly afterward (in Chapter 65), Amadís and his companions, while on their way from Lisuarte's court to the Ínsola Firme, meet the giant Madarque. Amadís defeats him and this causes a brief address by the author to the reader (also in Chapter 65) on how God overthrows the proud, for which he also, and again, adduces the case of Nimrod and the Tower of Babel—and some other unspecified biblical examples. These two cases of brief and passing authorial comment on subsidiary actions do, however, add to the accumulating body of moral thought applied to the narrative as it progresses. A rather long intervention occurs in Chapter 67. Here the author compares Florestán's forbearance in the battle with Lisuarte to Hector's with Ajax Telamon at Troy. But again this is not a substantial statement, and can also be seen as merely a case of bringing in a not very appropriate classical allusion for the sake of giving some prestige to the text.

Considerably later, at the end of the important Chapter 71, in which the boy Esplandián and his tutor Nasciano join Lisuarte at court and in which Oriana recognizes her own son, the author briefly and ironically reflects on the boy's unusual upbringing in the woods and with the lioness: "These are the wonders of that powerful God and keeper of all of us which he performs when it is His will, while other children of kings and great lords are reared in rich silks and among soft and delicate things; even with so much love of the person who rears them, with such comfort and care, even when those who have charge of them do not sleep or rest, yet with a small and insignificant accident they are taken out of the world" (III, 780). This little insertion by the author does at least make the valid point, in a story of action and violence, that life always has its chances and hazards, and he relates this to God's will.

Chapter 74 tells of Amadís's stay, as the Knight of the Green Sword, at the court of Constantinople, after he had won great fame in eastern Europe, culminating in the defeat of the dreaded Endriago. At this point the author makes an interesting general comment very much in keeping with the European views of class structure and social hierarchy of an age that still believed in aristocratic values. The reason for the comment was our hero's charm as a courtier and his constancy as a lover:

. . . they were very well impressed with the graceful replies given by the Knight of the Green Sword to all that they said to him; and thus this made them believe, even more than his great courage, that he was a man of high position. Courage and valor often occur in men of low kind and of coarse judgment but seldom do decent civility and polished breeding, since these belong to those who come from pure and noble blood. I do not say that all achieve this, but I do say that they should do so as something to which they are attached and placed under obligation, as has been the case with the Knight of the Green Sword, for, by placing a ring of great suffering and of commitment as a lover around the fierceness of his strong heart, he forbade both pride and anger to find a place in which to harm his high virtue. (III, 823)

We can also see here something of the moral balance and the graces required by an age which was to produce several manuals of courtly behavior, of which the *Amadís* itself, as has been stated, was to become one of the prime literary sources. The older medieval virtues of bravery and physical prowess were now tempered with gentility and breeding.

At the end of the same Chapter 74 the author makes a most severe condemnation of the emperor of Rome whose messengers had arrived to ask for Oriana's hand in marriage. Such an evil and unloved man can only be seen as somehow mad in believing that he could be loved by God; his sure fate was dishonor here and damnation afterward. This is the strongest and most partisan intervention so far of the author in the action of his own romance.

Soon, however, we get other uncompromising judgments and prophecies. There are two toward the end of Book III which are again clearly meant to underline the action at this point and how it is to lead to the calamities of Book IV. First, in Chapter 78, the author comments in passing on the "profía y riguridad" ("stubbornness and rigidity") of King Lisuarte. Even after his closest advisers urged him not to proceed with Oriana's marriage to El Patín, and even while ignoring all the prestige brought to him by Amadís, prestige greater than that of any monarch of his time, he was still to bring dishonor and loss upon himself, ironically as a result of the actions of this same loyal Amadís. Later, in Chapter 80, and as another anticipation of Book IV, the author returns to the same theme, namely, the stubbornness of Lisuarte, and states that an angry fortune which had raised him to such heights of success "was pleased, more for the restoration of his soul than of his honor, to change things around on him, as will be told to you in the Fourth Book of this great history, because there it will be set out at greater length" (III, 896).

Finally, and a very few pages later, also in Chapter 80, Book III is made to end on a more hopeful note (as had Book I). This very corrupted and ill-advised King Lisuarte displays his sense of gratitude and his loyalty to his old friend Grumedán, the tutor to Amadís's mother, by offering to fight beside him in his combat with the Romans. How fortunate, says our author, and it would seem ironically, are those vassals to whom God gives such kings prepared to offer them their own lives and possessions.

Once more we see how our author has isolated for comment incidents that bring out and emphasize what seems to be now the chief aspect of his moral ideas. He returns more than once to the

grievous sin of pride, especially its fateful example in the stubbornness of a very powerful and highly regarded monarch. Still, the
reader is also asked to consider such other lessons as forebearance in
battle, chance and God's will, the importance of breeding and its
moral value, as well as the virtues of gratitude and loyalty.

Book IV opens with the well-known author's comment about the
discovery of Book IV, and his praise of Esplandián and the latter's
great future as a Christian knight. It is worth noting that much of
this is irrelevant to Book IV itself, since Esplandián is to be the hero
of Book V, or the *Sergas*. Nevertheless, the fanciful discovery of
Book IV (echoing the similar statement in the prologue to Book I)
has its clear interest in trying to determine Montalvo's part in the
elaboration of the romance. The authorial comment on the action of
Book IV really begins, and very early, in Chapter 83, with a direct
rhetorical address to King Lisuarte, asking him to think again of his
great fortune and prestige as the "Señor . . . de cuallería" ("Lord
of chivalry"), and wondering if his loss of all this is in fact an act of
fortune or his own doing, which he will bitterly regret. Lisuarte
should, in blaming his fortune, also blame his own ill judgment of
men and his hardheartedness in dealing with his own daughter. The
pithy and vivid conclusion runs thus: ". . . so that if fortune by
turning its wheel should be your opponent, you have untied it from
where it was attached" (IV, 964).

Thus at the outset of this final book, so full of action and crises, the
stage is set and the moral position is made clear. This important
restatement of the destructiveness of Lisuarte and its likely consequences is soon followed by an equally significant harangue of
Amadís (in Chapter 85) to his knights in the Ínsola Firme, recalling
to the reader the one delivered in Book III before the battle with
Salustanquidio and the rescue of Oriana. Again stressing their duties
and outlining the distressing position created by Lisuarte and El
Patín, Amadís gets their support, although another appeal will now
be made to the king.

Following closely on the heels of these preparations for the narrative climaxes (and as the opening of Chapter 87), there comes
another strikingly constructed passage, with rhetorical questions.
Here the author ponders and praises the loving service of so many
knights to Oriana, only because she was "the gentlest and of best
breeding and courtesy and above all of the most moderate humility
to be found in their time" (IV, 979). This peerless lady is exalted at

the outset of events that will test all the chief protagonists, and she is contrasted with those presumptuous lords who scorn the service and win the contempt of the people who would serve them.

Between the two tremendous battles, fought between Lisuarte and El Patín, on the one hand, and Amadís and his followers, on the other, together with all their respective allies ("no el mundo mas todo lo más de la cristiandad y la flor della estaua allí"—"not the world but most of Christendom and the flower of it was there"), there is sandwiched another set of reflections (in Chapter 111), on the now familiar and recurring theme of human folly and its consequences. Many innocent will die in these conflicts, although they may also save their souls. On the other hand, "thus it can be counted as a greater and more dangerous death, even if at present they still have their lives, for those who cause such destruction as that occasioned by King Lisuarte although he was very prudent and knowledgeable in all things, as you have heard. This came about through his not wishing to take counsel from anyone but himself" (IV, 1108). Thus, it is clearly implied, may a good man bring about his own undoing.

Just after this, as the second battle ends, the author reflects (at the very end of the same Chapter 111) on how love is greater than all other things, since Amadís, whose love for Oriana (Lisuarte's daughter) is a main theme of the romance, now calls a halt to the slaughter and thus saves the king. The conclusion is again in keeping with the author's philosophy of events, since this truce will lead to great and eventual peace, and it is clearly the work of "aquel Señor que es reparador de todas las cosas" ("of that Lord who is repairer of all things"). We have here a moral as well as a narrative climax.

Again the author inserts in passing a compensatory example of Lisuarte's good nature (see the case in Chapter 80 of Book III), when he frees King Cildadán from his vassalage, taking the intention for the deed (in Chapter 112). Nevertheless, a little later on (in Chapter 116), the author once more returns to a consideration, again couched in telling rhetorical questions, of the deserts of the king. This time, and as Lisuarte is on the point of defeat at Lubaina, the author spells out once more in full how he listened to Brocadán and Gandandel and turned against Amadís who had brought him so much fame. He asks sarcastically what fate his so-called allies would have brought him but his own end, just like that of Arcaláus, Arábigo, and Barsinán. Amadís certainly owed him nothing and yet he will save him once more, since our hero "no pensaua sino en autos nobles" ("only thought in terms of noble acts"). This clear contrast brings Lisuarte to the point of lowest esteem in these continuing comments, and raises Amadís to an even higher level of magnanimity.

The good knight Grumedán, when this last awful battle is over and peace is made between Lisuarte and Amadís, himself comments, almost like the voice of the author, on the evil of Arcaláus and how we can all learn from his fearful example (see Chapter 117). A counterpart of this last is a true authorial comment (at the end of Chapter 117), when judgment is passed on the election of El Patín's successor as emperor of Rome, namely, the good Arquisil, who survived injustices and exile from his predecessor. It would appear that sometimes it is better to be subject to good people than to use our freedom to serve evil, "porque de lo bueno bueno se espera en la fin, . . . y de lo malo, . . . ahunque algún tiempo tenga flores, al cabo han de ser secas las rosas" ("because good is expected from good at the end, . . . but as for evil, . . . even if for some time it may produce flowers, finally the roses will dry up"). This reflection makes strange reading, if it is seen merely in a modern political context as a defense of the good dictator. If, however, it is related to a paternalistic, feudal society, its meaning becomes clear. As another assessment of the abuse of power and its outcome, its place in rounding off one of the main narrative strands of the *Amadís* (that concerning the Romans) is of special significance.

From this point the romance continues to tie up many other narrative ends and thus much comment by the characters themselves arises naturally from the story, that is, as events draw to their close and thus allow assessment of achievements. The author himself fittingly uses the advanced stage of fulfillment of the story to reflect on the one relationship that has survived unblemished, namely, the passion of Amadís and Oriana (he does so in Chapter 130, and again at the beginning of a chapter). This, even when Amadís had his beloved in his possession, continued to grow, unlike other loves that wax and wane, because it was a pure love and founded on virtue. He goes on to reflect in general on how satiety can lead to vexatiousness and the sweet can become bitter, and again how we tend to follow the easy path of pleasure which leads to repentence rather than that of the good which, while itself leading us through hardships, brings final happiness. Amadís and Oriana, however, are an exceptional case of love; they overcame their many "cuydados y angustias" ("cares and anguishes") because of the steadfastness and purity of their attachment. Their love is in fact described in the fashion of much contemporary European poetry (and much also of the neo-Petrarchan manner of the sixteenth century), although this is the rare case of triumphant love: "because, while as often as they brought their great love to their memories, so often did they have each other in front of their eyes, as if in fact this was taking place. This gave them such a great remedy and such consolation for their happy anxieties [that is, for anxieties that could thus be borne easily] that they wished in no way to let that sweet memory depart from them" (IV, 1286). One need do no more here than note a final underlining of a major area of significance in the *Amadís*, the true love of the hero for his lady. The romance's great European fame owed much to this main aspect of the novel, which was often read as a love story.

Authorial comments come to a close in the last four chapters with two sets of reflections again suitably affirmative in nature and both illustrative of the positive side of knightly conduct which has been upheld throughout the work. First, Galaor, now king of Sobradisa as husband of the beautiful Briolanja, is praised (still in Chapter 130) for his exemplary sense of duty in deciding to return to arms to help his cousin Dragonís. Galaor realizes that "la honrra no tiene cabo y . . . es tan delicada que con muy poco oluido se puede escurecer" ("honor has no ending, and . . . it is so delicate that with even a little forgetfulness it can be darkened"), and all knights are now asked to follow his example and not to rest on their laurels and thus lose what they have won.

Second, and finally (in Chapter 133), the author considers the last crisis caused by the sudden snatching away of Lisuarte. The latter is now once more reestablished in London ("la cabeça de todo el reyno"—"the head of all the kingdom"), as a noble king, for whom, as their defender, all his people now express their grief. Queen Brisena asks for the help of Amadís and his knights who at once respond: "Oh how fortunate monarchs should consider themselves if their vassals with such love and great grief should regret their losses and hardships; and when indeed there should be vassals who both could and should feel thus, would that too there should be monarchs acting toward their vassals as this noble king does to his!" (IV, 1330).

Times may be bad and standards forgotten, but it is to be hoped that God will produce better subjects and kings. The story has come full circle and the once erring monarch can now once more call on the support of all. This last comment shows how Lisuarte has been conceived as a rounded human being, with virtues and faults, and also allows the author (as he now does) to end his long story by striking again the necessary note of preparation for the succession of Amadís's son, Esplandián. The latter (made a knight by Urganda at the end of Chapter 133) in fact frees the captive Lisuarte, not in the *Amadís*, but in Chapter 6 of the *Sergas*, which itself ends with a mysterious enchantment of its main characters.

To sum up: the interlarding of the narrative of the *Amadís* with moralistic comments is, as we have seen, a method of interpreting actions and events, prospectively and retrospectively (thus recalling certain purely narrative devices). For all we know, these comments may be the work of Montalvo; most probably he is the author of those occurring in Books III and IV, in which all critics agree his hand can most clearly be seen (Dr. Mottola for one has noted, for example, their increasing use in the last two books). Further, Montalvo's Book V, or the *Sergas*, explicitly and systematically presents its hero, Amadís's son and successor, as the prototype of the Christian knight. These authorial intercalations fulfill both an ideological and a structural function. They break up or interrupt the long story and give pause to the reader, who is asked to consider the meaning or import of the text. Some other long narratives of the same general period of the printed *Amadís*, for example the *Orlando furioso* of Ariosto, were to be subjected to a much more rigorous, if extratextual, moral commentary by the use of *allegorie*, or prose allegorical explanations, thus continuing in a new form a very long tradition of moralizing of poetic and other literary texts.[4]

The other obvious point to be made is that the practice of commenting on historical events is also very old and goes back at least to the historical and other books of the Old Testament, where we meet with many references to the pride of the mighty and its dire consequences. This practice, like that of allegorism, continued up to the end of the Middle Ages and after. In the Spanish chronicles themselves Montalvo would have found examples of this moralism ready to hand, especially in reasonably contemporary historical biographies, in which the subject was seen as representing certain categories of moral choice. More than one critic has rightly pointed to the influence on our romance and its fellows of the tradition of historical prose, with which certain parallels with the techniques of the *Amadís* can be found, although it is worth stating again that, however much the early novel owes to the prior genre of historiography, there are essential differences between the recording and interpreting of fact and the writing of fiction.

In addition, and, as Miss G. Williams first suggested, we should consider that the author of the *Amadís* made use of such a work as Colonna's on princes and public power or of one of its Castilian adaptations, such as that of García de Castrojeriz, who (as we stated in Chapter 3 above) made the first known reference to our romance. Such political doctrine permeated writing at a time when many tried to reconcile Christian belief with the realities of power, and it is not at all surprising that the *Amadís* should concern itself to such an extent with this general topic. There would not therefore seem to be much point in searching for the specific sources of the author's thought. However unoriginal the latter may be, there can be no doubt that it forms an important element in the elaboration of the material of our romance.

The *Amadís* then, and almost as if it were the chronicle of a single monarch or prince, is to be seen as illustrating both the responsibilities of public life and the conduct of the princely individual. We witness the dedication and loyalty of Amadís as knight and courtier as well as the esteem in which King Lisuarte is, at least at first, held as the greatest monarch in Christendom. These two figures, around whom most of the action increasingly revolves, are, however, pitted against one another largely because of Lisuarte's gullibility and pride. The comments thus uncover the narrative spine or the ideological core of the action and give the latter a meaning in terms of human motives and conduct. Amadís is, of course, not alone Lisuarte's one-time faithful champion and his later reluctant enemy, but also his daughter's lover and eventually Lisuarte's own successor.

The comments can concern themselves with small if typical happenings or with the events of central importance. They reveal the chivalric virtues of loyalty, bravery, good breeding, and, of course, true love for one's lady, with, in addition, love's heartbreaks and hardships. The comments also clearly reflect the corresponding practice in this kind of moralism (often, as stated above, with rhetorical forms) of using events to praise or to blame, to commend or to condemn.

Underlying and explicitly informing the comments to the *Amadís* is a simple but repeated statement concerning God's omnipotence, His grace and His mysterious ways, and the relation of these things to the salvation or damnation of one's soul. In the most obvious sense, therefore, it is true to say that the romance is a work written firmly within a Christian context. We shall later see how pervasive and varied are the reflections of religion in the *Amadís*.

IV *Related Devices*

We have now seen, in the above examination of the text, some of the ways by which the abundant material of the *Amadís* is set out with an eye to readability and with the object of making the reader ponder its meaning. Other related devices or features, likewise reflecting contemporary rules of writing, further illustrate the author's endeavors to bring variety to the narrative. Some of these other features also have the effect of placing the lover-hero in a setting reminiscent of the sentimental novel with its despairs and self-analysis.

Thus our romance has several striking cases of the use of monologues or soliloquies placed in the mouths of the characters; these are rhetorical features closely allied, of course, to the authorial interventions in content and manner of presentation. The *Amadís* also makes use of letters, themselves a rhetorical feature to be found in contemporary fiction. Early in Book II, at the beginning of Chapter 46, Amadís, suffering from the terrible impact of Oriana's letter (quoted in Chapter 44), and before he, ironically, defeats El Patín (Oriana's later unwanted suitor), gives voice to no fewer than five soliloquies expressing his agony, in the tortured suicidal manner typical of the conventions of courtly love. These outbursts, which are brief but once more couched in vigorous oratorical style, are addressed to Fortune, Oriana, King Perión, Gandales, his cousin Mabilia, and the Damsel of Denmark. This kind of monologue has its psychological as well as its structural importance and gives the proper emphasis to the great crisis in the young Amadís's career.

In passing, reference should be made to another narrative variation (in Chapter 51), again typical of the sentimental novel and of its witty and involved expression, namely, Amadís's song of despair in the wilderness (this, it will be recalled, is the only piece of verse in the whole novel apart from Leonoreta's little song, which became a subject of so much argument):

> Since victory is denied to me
> where by right it was due,
> there where glory dies
> it is glory for life to die.
>
> And with this death of mine
> all my harms will die,
> my hope, my persistence,
> love and its deceptions;
> but there will remain in my memory
> the never lost pity,
> for through killing my glory
> they killed for me both glory and life
>
> (II,414)

This is followed (in Chapter 52) by Oriana's second letter asking forgiveness. This, of course, brings Amadís's self-imposed exile to an end and his return to Oriana. Later (in Chapter 56) the author makes Amadís once more into the contemplative (as against the commonly combative) figure, when he sits by a stream and again considers, in the form of an indirect soliloquy, such things as variable fortune, God's grace, his love for Oriana, and man's perishable estate.

Other letters follow. Urganda, the good woman magician, sends epistles to King Lisuarte and to Amadís's brother Galaor (Chapter 57), warning them both to be careful of what may befall them in the coming great battle with King Cildadán—this latter is to live to fight another day, for Lisuarte against Amadís! Thus this device is used as a kind of prophecy of action. Another ally of Lisuarte, King Arbán of North Wales, also writes to Lisuarte (at the end of Chapter 57), telling how he and Angriote are in the painful captivity of Mongaça. Although their liberation has to await events, the letter is used here for yet another purpose, that of increasing the narrative tension.

Book IV presents us, for example, with the case of Amadís's harangue (in Chapter 85), which recalls the shorter speeches by Count Argamón (in Chapter 78) and Amadís himself (in Chapter 80), since they all deal with Lisuarte's obduracy and the impending great conflict. Now Amadís praises his knights for their service and asks their advice. Quadragante answers for them all, supporting and approving his last-minute pleas to Lisuarte to accept peace and justice. This harangue and its answer make up almost all of a very short chapter, thus drawing attention to their function as a signpost in the narrative. Other such speeches and addresses by other characters occur in successive chapters, when missions seek help from several different courts and monarchs. (The rather long statement by a single character is also a common feature of the *Amadís*.) Thus in Chapter 89 Amadís speaks the contents of a letter which Gandalín is to take to Perión asking for his aid. There is also Oriana's letter to her mother Queen Brisena (in Chapter 95) asking for her intercession with Lisuarte. Much later, and after all the fighting and destruction are over (and they and the preparation for them take up much of the middle portion of Book IV), the holy man Nasciano thanks God in a public prayer for the peace now reached (in Chapter 117), thus providing an example of a very old and common narrative "interruption."[5]

Urganda's final appearance in the story, which effectively stretches over the last ten chapters, ends with her disappearance, and the discovery by Amadís of her final letter (in Chapter 133). This feature serves in this case the purpose of drawing the *Amadís* to a close and of preparing the way for the continuation by Esplandián. Amadís and his companions are asked to be content with their achievements and to govern their subjects in peace, leaving the future to their younger successors, and Urganda says that, in a sense, it will be said that the son killed the father. (This of course is the phrase commented on by those critics searching for the dimensions and the content of the primitive *Amadís*.)

Any detailed account of the structural features of the *Amadís* should include some mention of the use of the related devices of secrecy and discovery. These are, of course, to be found in a very great deal of fiction but they play a particularly important role in our romance, as in its Breton models, and, in fact, as already indicated, discovery can also constitute an element of interweaving.

From the very outset, secrecy enters our story. Thus Amadís's birth and origins are, as we know, not immediately made public. This naturally provides the kind of narrative delay and suspense that arouses expectancy and pleasure in the reader. Perión and Elisena have good reasons for keeping their marriage secret (in Chapter 1), that is, because of his departure and the so-called law of Scotland. The same (at the end of this chapter) applies to their son's birth and his dispatch, with a brief and not very explicit letter, on the open sea. Perión soon after (in Chapter 4) solemnly dubs his (unknown) son a knight at the request of Amadís's new love, Oriana, and this happens just before Amadís, like another Lancelot, expresses a wish to know his origins. Soon after this again (also in Chapter 4), as Amadís is about to leave Oriana, she asks him whose son he is, since she is sure he is not Gandales's and Amadís replies with what he had heard from King Languines.

Thus it goes on, as Amadís shows himself more and more to be the outstanding knight he is: Oriana hides well her secret love for Amadís (in Chapter 7), while, as she leaves Languines's court for that of her father, Lisuarte, she discovers the letter from Amadís's ark which tells her his true name and that he is a king's son; this she sends to him and he receives it (in Chapter 9), greatly overjoyed to know his name and his royal origins. When Amadís first arrives in Gaul (in Chapter 8), his mother Elisena admires him as she recalls her lost sons, that is, Amadís and Galaor, not knowing that he is one of them; very soon afterward (in Chapter 10) Amadís's ring and sword and the same letter reveal to Perión and Elisena that he is their son; this is later confirmed to Amadís by Gandalín in Chapter 15. Not long after this again (in Chapter 11), through Oriana's intercession, Galaor gets to know Amadís as his brother and also who his parents are. Other significant cases of revelation and secrecy in Book I are the near mortal combat, instigated by Arcaláus's niece, between Amadís and Galaor and stopped in time by Baláys de Carsante who tells them who they are (in Chapter 22); Galaor's recognition of the love between Amadís and Oriana (in Chapter 30); and Galaor's discovery that his opponent is his half brother and subsequent companion in arms, Florestán (in Chapter 41).

Apart from the love of Amadís and Oriana, kept secret for so long, another important disguise resulting in much secrecy and its eventual revelation is, of course, that of Amadís when (in Chapter 48) he retires temporarily from the world as the hermit Beltenebrós. Even after he emerges from the Peña Pobre, Amadís hides his identity by keeping his new name and keeping his helmet on (in Chapter 55), as he travels to Oriana, and when he sends Quadragante and two giants as captives to King Lisuarte, thus causing the comment that Beltenebrós's deeds are greater than Amadís's, and creating a kind of dual personality for himself (in the same chapter and in Chapter 56). Then, of course, both he, as Beltenebrós, and Oriana, with a mask, go disguised to Lisuarte's court and pass Macandón's tests of the sword and the headdress, while they also keep their identity from Enil, Gandales's nephew, and Amadís's squires (also in Chapter 56 and in Chapter 57). Amadís's apparently

separate identity from Beltenebrós arouses the jealousy of his
brothers because of the latter's fame in arms, although this ends
when Amadís, in the heat of the great battle between Cildadán and
Lisuarte, reveals his true identity (Chapters 57 and 58), although
Galaor does not hear the news till his temporary captivity by Urganda (in Chapter 59). Even after this Oriana keeps secret her love
for Amadís when she and Briolanja discuss the results of the battle
(in Chapter 58), while Urganda, on her visit to Lisuarte's court (in
Chapter 60) assures Oriana that she will not reveal her love for
Amadís. The Enchantress's activities and those of Arcaláus, which
involve prophecy, interpretation of events, secrecy, and revelation,
will be examined later.

Amadís continues to keep his love a secret from his close companions in arms (in the unnumbered first chapter of Book III), from
his cousin Agrajes when (in Chapter 63) they go under the Lovers'
Arch in the Ínsola Firme, and from his dear brother Galaor, despite
the latter's protest (in Chapter 65). A happy revelation, and reunion,
occurs when (in the same chapter) Elisena and Perión, with great
emotion, meet Amadís and Galaor, as they reach Gaul. Book III also
contains the loss of the baby Esplandián to the lioness and the
peasants, a fact which both Mabilia and the youth Durín hide from
Oriana (in Chapter 66). There follows the child's discovery and
baptism by the holy man Nasciano (in the same chapter). At this
point too Perión meets his natural son Florestán for the first time (in
Chapter 68), and then he and his three sons decide to go to the help
of Lisuarte against Arcaláus and Arábigo (in the same chapter),
although they are at variance with him; they do so incognito by
using arms given to them for the occasion by Urganda's damsel (in
the same chapter). Just after this battle (in Chapter 69), Perión,
Amadís, and the others discover that the lady saved by them from
Arcaláus's castle is the person who had cast Amadís into the sea as a
child. This narrative throwback is a special kind of revelation, recalling, as stated before, the methods of interweaving, and is
paralleled much later in the *Amadís* when, toward the end (in
Chapter 127), Amadís discovers that the lady in distress he is helping is in fact Darioleta, his mother Elisena's former damsel, who had
brought her and Perión together and arranged for Amadís's dispatch
on the sea.

Later in Book III (Chapter 71), Esplandián and Nasciano meet
Lisuarte and his retinue and, as we know, the boy is brought to

court where he is recognized by his mother Oriana, who also reveals her secret marriage to the holy man, who in his turn then absolves her of sin. When after his period of unhappy idleness, Amadís leaves Gaul and goes east into central Europe and the Balkans, he does so as the Knight of the Green Sword, a pseudonym and disguise, its implications maintained throughout this series of episodes. For example, Amadís keeps the name of Oriana from the emperor and empress and the Princess Leonorina in Constantinople (in Chapter 74), despite their endeavors to find out about his beloved. This secrecy fits in with Amadís's own anonymity here, but it also recalls Amadís's and Oriana's continuing wish not to reveal their love publicly, an attitude generally reminiscent of the world of courtly love, although, as will be stated again, their love was neither adulterous nor otherwise improper. The conflict between Amadís and Lisuarte prevented early revelation, as did the subsequent role of Oriana as a kind of pawn or counter in the war between one side and the other. Even when Amadís informs his Greek hosts that he knows about Apolidón, the emperor's grandfather, and the lord of the Ínsola Firme, and thus Amadís's predecessor there (in the same chapter), Amadís still hides his identity. He went away from Oriana for five years and tried to build for himself a new career, although ironically his former fame went before him, as when King Trafinor recalls to him Amadís's deeds (in Chapter 70). Thus Amadís's former feats become entangled with his new achievements, as we have also seen happen when he went under the name of Beltenebrós.

His identity continues to be hidden as he sets out, to return to Oriana, in the ship with the beautiful Princess Grasinda, and, as he approaches Great Britain (in Chapter 78), he begs his companions to call him the Greek Knight, since he knows well that he might be recognized by his sword were he still to take it for his nickname. Towards the end of Book III (in Chapter 80), when Amadís and his company reach the end of their voyage, he is compelled to reveal his identity to Grasinda, when he is received in the Ínsola Firme as its lord (a fact of which she was of course already aware). Not long after (in Chapter 88) he must also reveal himself in asking for the help of the emperor of Constantinople in the coming struggle. An ironic consequence of Amadís's long disguise is found in Grasinda's account to Oriana and Briolanja of how she could not win his heart (in Chapter 92).

The later chapters of Book IV contain a spate of revelations of old secrets, as one might expect from a story as it runs out. Thus (in Chapter 113), when Nasciano, with Esplandián's help, begins the final moves toward peace and reconciliation, he tells Lisuarte of Amadís's and Oriana's early secret marriage (to be commented on later); just after this Amadís is greatly overjoyed to recognize Esplandián as his son, while Nasciano also (in the same chapter) informs Amadís that he too knew it all before. As this important piece of information concerning Esplandián (who at the very end of the romance is raised up as the new future hero) comes late to Amadís, the latter, on finding (in Chapter 117) that Lisuarte already also knew of it, reacts by blushing. As stated before, Urganda herself later makes significant revelations, but these will also be looked at below. Very much toward the end, as we know, there is the late dramatic reappearance (in Chapter 127) of Darioleta, Queen Elisena's maid, who now reveals herself to Amadís as he sets out to help her.

Several other cases of revelation and secrecy occur in the narrative. It is hoped, however, that the above examples will adequately illustrate a device which, like other elements in the *Amadís* yet to be analyzed, forms part of the very texture of the novel. Like other structural features it introduces variety and suspense, and this keeps the appetite whetted and the story going. It need only be said that as a dual feature it is as old as storytelling itself and still plays a vital part in the human condition and its portrayal in literature.

As far as structural divisions are concerned, the above coverage of devices and of features might conclude with a few words on the use of dialogue or conversation in the romance. This, a most common feature in any piece of modern fiction, finds its place in the *Amadís* and in fact is used throughout. It is largely employed, however, to permit a character to ask a question or to give an order, or to perform briefly the clarificatory function of explaining or anticipating actions, and further it normally occurs in short spurts between two or three people. It thus seldom if ever takes on the role of a true conversation, but nevertheless it does serve the real purpose of bringing the narrative alive and of giving further variety to the overall action of the story. Dialogue in the *Amadís* exists as a minor but persistent component side by side with the equally prevalent long statement or monologue, with the account, long or short, of a sudden action, the more detached relation of events, and the recurring devices and features mentioned above. In this respect the comparative subservience of dialogue in our romance differs from its more significant use in the pastoral novel or indeed in *Don Quixote* and many later forms of the novel. Here it was to be developed as the vehicle of psychological analysis or revelation of character, and even to become an animated substitute for description or straight narrative.

Before leaving this account of some of the details of the structure of the *Amadís*, a reference should be made again to its main lines of narrative progression and its climaxes. These have been indicated in the earlier summary of the plot and have also been mentioned in the above analyses. Suffice it to say here that the author makes much use of rhetorical devices, by listing lords, knights, and their lands and hosts, to prepare the reader for the great moments, and, as we have seen, by the use of soliloquies, disquisitions, and letters, to emphasize their significance. These climaxes are the London assemblies in Book I, and in Book II the break between Oriana and Amadís and his subsequent but temporary exile, together with the poisoning of Lisuarte's mind by his courtiers, and Amadís's departure from his court. The progress of Amadís to eastern Europe and the climaxes of his struggle with the Endriago and his triumphant arrival in Constantinople, the sea battle against Salustanquidio and the rescue of Oriana, all come in Book III; and then the deliberate and well-orchestrated buildup to the final battles with Lisuarte and El Patín, the many reconciliations, marriages, and settlements, belong to Book IV. In all this, other special creations and devices, such as Urganda, the good fairy and the *dea ex machina*, or the Ínsola Firme and the lovers' tests, with their strategic recurrence, also keep reminding the reader of the ebbing and flowing of events and of their due progression to the end, as well as their underlying meaning.

In other words, a consideration of the articulated use of devices can again lay bare the main disposal through crises and climaxes of the whole romance. We have seen, in a little detail, how some of this is done. We shall now continue to look at the contents of the *Amadís* under other, sometimes related, headings. This, it is hoped, will further illustrate the riches of its structure and the variety of its subject matter.

CHAPTER 5

The Characters, Their Habits, and Their Beliefs

I Varieties and Classes

STRUCTURE and contents cannot, of course, always be satisfactorily separated, and it will already be clear that the *Amadís*, like other long works of fiction, partly owes its success to a fusion of both. It is now proposed to look at some other aspects of the subject matter, although this further incursion into the heart of the romance will not always necessarily involve considerations of structure.

More than one critic has drawn attention to the abundance of characters and of place-names in the *Amadís*, and special interest has been aroused in their etymological and other origins.[1] Here Amadís and his many fellows and their wanderings will be taken for granted, but some attempt will be made to see them in their variety, to examine their conduct and reactions, and to fit them into the social dispensation portrayed in the work. Later, the setting of the *Amadís*, that is, its geography, physical background and their presentation, will be considered separately.

There is a total of some two hundred seventy characters altogether in our romance. This figure excludes nicknames for characters otherwise named and also persons from the ancient world, the Bible, or the Arthurian tradition, but it includes those playing the smallest roles as well as the main protagonists. This raw total will perhaps give some idea of how pervasive is the use of names in the *Amadís*, throughout which we are thus seen to be introduced to a large gallery of people often connected or related to one another. There can be no doubt that nomenclature serves both to identify people and places and to enrich the story, thus producing an effect of moving along a tapestry or wandering at large in a seemingly endless social pageant.

Many of the types from the *Amadís* belong to a tradition established in the earlier romances, but, it should be stressed again, the moral universe of our romance is markedly different when it comes to the central love story or when we consider the increasing emphasis upon the Christian duties of the knights. From the outset we find ourselves in a monarchical and aristocratic world, and thus the dynastic position is early set out. Amadís is the son of Perión, king of Gaul, and of Elisena, daughter of the king of Little Britain, while Oriana is the daughter of Lisuarte (who has succeeded his brother Falangrís as king of Great Britain), and of Brisena, daughter of the king of Denmark. As a result of Amadís's secret birth, following his parents' "secret marriage", we soon meet King Languines of Scotland, at whose court Amadís is presented by his foster father, the Scottish knight Gandales, who rears Amadís with his own son Gandalín, who in turn is to become Amadís's most loyal squire. At this point too there appears Urganda the Unknown, who is to be the beneficent fairy, protectress, and prophetess throughout the romance but who, we are assured, is also subject to God's will. (Lisuarte is to remark of her later, in Chapter 71: "La sabiduría desta muger no se puede pensar ni escreuir," that is, "this woman's wisdom cannot be conceived or written about.")

The social scene has been further filled out with the appearance of Darioleta, confidante of Elisena, and of Amadís's cousin Mabilia and the Damsel of Denmark, both of whom become Oriana's damsels in waiting. Also, Amadís is soon to have a brother, Galaor, and his twin sister, Melicia, and Galaor is to be carried off, because of a prophecy, by the first of the giants, Gandalás of Leonís, who has his little captive reared by a hermit.[2] All this has taken place in the first three chapters. Soon, when Amadís is knighted, he is joined by his other cousin, Agrajes, with whom he defeats King Abiés of Ireland who is attacking Gaul. It is, of course, in the nature of the tale at this stage and for most of Book I, with its succession of characters, that Amadís should meet many new people, knights, ladies, and damsels, some of whom appear in groups, in a host, or at an assembly or court. Thus as he sets out for Lisuarte's court in Windsor to meet Oriana he encounters Galaor for the first time (he too joins Agrajes as one of Amadís's companions) and Urganda for the second time.

Evil figures there also are. Of the latter the evil enchanter of the *Amadís*, a kind of devilish counterpart of Urganda, is Arcaláus, who is to dog Amadís's progress, particularly in Book IV. Arcaláus's companions in intrigue include the usurper King Barsinán, lord of Sansueña, and Arábigo, also a king. Another evil man, who appears early but lasts for only a short time, is Dardán the Haughty. By the end of Book I we have in addition met a new set of people in Queen Briolanja and her circle, especially the other usurper, King Abíseos, whom Amadís defeats and kills, and Amadís's Spanish cousin, Brián of Monjaste. By now too Amadís has been joined by Angriote and Bruneo and he will meet his own half brother, Florestán, son of Perión and of the unnamed daughter of the Count of Zeeland, and to these will be added later still others like Quadragante, brother of Abiés. Thus Amadís's company of faithful knights and companions in trials and victory will be completed.

To the characters of the court and of public affairs and those involved in the many combats, there should be added another category which is to play a significant role throughout the romance, namely, the men of religion. Thus we have come across the "hermitaño, buen hombre de santa vida" ("the hermit, a good man of holy life"), who is entrusted by the giant Gandalás with Galaor's education. We recall that the same kind of arrangement is made (in Book III) for Esplandián, also carried off as a child, who is partly reared by foster parents (as was his own father) but also by the most famous holy man of all, Nasciano, who is to become the peacemaker in Book IV. This kind of person, for whom, both as a tutor and as a king's adviser, historical parallels are not lacking, is apparently conceived as outside the social hierarchy. There are in addition many cases in the *Amadís* in which a hermit and his humble dwelling provide rest, cure, and food for knights on their way from one adventure to another. Thus (as early as Chapter 11) we find Galaor, on his way to win back Gandalás's castle from the evil giant Albadán, staying the night with a hermit ("de orden"; that is, of a religious order), who tries to dissuade him from his attempt but gives him shelter and, having said mass for him, agrees to pray for his success. These minor characters also help to connect one episode with another or to bridge the different parts of a single episode, and it is also to be noted that those dedicated to the solitary religious life support the actions of the good knight. This again reflects the alliance and even the identification of religion and secular power in medieval society.

Other different types who serve and help the great also appear at an early stage (the *doncellas* should be excluded from this category because of their special position as ladies in waiting). Thus a squire reminds Galaor (in Chapter 15) of his limited position by saying that he cannot yet fight as a knight. Amadís, on his first adventures (in Chapters 17 and 19), twice stays the night with an "infançón" (gentleman of the lower nobility), while (in Chapter 17) our hero takes as a guide the dwarf Ardián, who is to serve his master well in many episodes. Baláys, another knightly supporter of Amadís, and a damsel spend the night (in Chapter 28) at the house of "dos dueñas que santa vida hazían" ("two ladies living a saintly life"), and share their poor fare and receive their thanks for defeating the marauding thieves. Once more Amadís and Galaor (in Chapter 33) spend the night, on their way to Lisuarte's court in London, with a hermit, where "ouieron muy pobre cena" ("where they dined very meagerly").

Later (in Chapter 36) Galaor, passing through a forest, a very typical setting for such a happening, comes into the open and meets up with some muleteers who feed his horse and give him a place to sleep. In Chapter 35 some woodcutters ("villanos," or villeins), who had seen both Lisuarte and Oriana being taken by Arcaláus, inform Amadís and his knights of this; another hermit at this point also gives them helpful advice. Later (in Chapter 37) these same woodcutters come to London and tell Queen Brisena. Thus the humble folk of the novel, just like Amadís's dwarf in Chapter 40, when he wrongly suggests to Oriana that Amadís loves Briolanja, now inadvertently cause distress, when they bring news that Lisuarte and Oriana are still Aracaláus's captives after they have in fact been freed. Not always it seems do they play a supporting role, as it were, but on certain occasions can be said to divert or redirect the main action of the story. At the end of Chapter 39, the badly wounded knight Olivas is brought from the scene of combat to Lisuarte's own dwelling, where he is left in the care of "maestros," or physicians, to cure him, with, as is said, God's help. These medical attendants appear frequently, as might be expected, fulfilling an important minor role, while adding a touch of realism to the many horrific encounters and battles of the *Amadís*.

Book I again provides features which can be seen to be typical of the romance as a whole. The social setting is drawn in a linear rather than in any deep fashion, but this is surely appropriate for a novel of continuous action in which the characters are almost all types, clearly if superficially identified, and not needing any great analysis for their acceptance. There are, however, apart from Lisuarte and Amadís, cases of personal decision in interpreting codes of behavior which tend to turn types into characters, and some of these will be noted below when their conduct and habits are considered. The range of social coverage is limited also for good reasons, given the subject of the *Amadís*, but the lower orders do exist in their own right as suppliers and helpers, mostly to fill the gaps, often nocturnal, between one adventure and another. This coverage also explains in its own way why the main characters, with power and position and realizable ambitions, emerge naturally at times to symbolize human virtues and vices. Their lowly fellow beings by contrast never reveal such propensities. It is as already stated very much an aristocrat's world that we encounter in the *Amadís*; yet we recall the author's special appeal to the lesser folk, in Chapter 42, as counselors to the great.

A more selective look at the other books will show some fresh variations on the pattern of Book I. Starting from below this time, we soon meet (in Chapter 48) a poorly dressed old religious, "hombre de orden," watering his horse, who tells Amadís that he is also "de missa," that is, he can say mass, and thus also hear Amadís's confession. This common recurrence of religious practice and profession will be commented on later. Further on in the same chapter, when Amadís as Beltenebrós is retiring voluntarily to the Peña Pobre, this same hermit, Andalod, arranges for him to be given his hermit's clothes by the boatmen who also row him out to the rock. Oriana, in her preparations at Miraflores to receive Amadís (in Chapter 53), approves of the spoken support received from the porter, who is on guard as a lookout, saying that Amadís is beloved even of "los hombres simples que de las cosas poco conoscimiento han" ("of simple men with little knowledge of affairs"); that is, she voices a sincere and in no sense patronizing view as from an exalted mistress about her servants. In the following chapter, a "niña," or little girl, acts as a messenger of important news at Miraflores.

At the level of the monarchy and the aristocratic circles which provide the characters who cause and control the actions of the romance, Book II expands the scene with the Ínsola Firme and its original conquerors and rulers, Apolidón and his wife Grimanesa, later emperor and empress of Greece. We also meet Oriana's young sister Leonoreta, for whom Amadís writes his little, and much discussed, song, and who later marries the emperor of Rome. Two human types of unrelieved evil are Brocadán and Gandandel, counselors of Lisuarte and instigators of the latter's folly and comparable in presentation and intention to Arcaláus. There is another (bad) giant, Famongomadán, killed by Amadís, and his daughter, the beautiful Madasima, who eventually marries Galvanes, but not before (in Book III) Amadís and Lisuarte fall out and a battle is fought on the matter. Book II also introduces us to Cildadán, husband of Abiés's daughter and also a king of Ireland, who fights Lisuarte and Amadís, is cured by Urganda, and eventually remains loyal to Lisuarte in the later battles.

Book III, as we already know, covers the birth of Esplandián and the first appearance of Nasciano. Amadís's son, whose rearing is also clandestine in its way, stands for the renewal of the dynasty and is soon to be restored to his inheritance and recognized at least by his mother. The role of the tame lioness, over which Nasciano has an Orpheus-like power, and which steals the infant Esplandián and later becomes his companion, retains its own symbolism of strength and purity from earlier literature. A whole new set of characters comes into the story with Amadís's travels abroad: King Trafinor of Bohemia, Prince Grasandor, Princess Grasinda, the emperor and empress of Constantinople and their daughter Leonorina (the future wife of Esplandián), the great physician and "maestro" Elisabad, who cures Amadís of his fearful wounds after he defeats the worst of all the giants, the Endriago (in Chapter 73). The latter creature has been prefigured in earlier examples of human monsters, such as Madarque, defeated and made a Christian by Amadís (in Chapter 65), and the frightful and elusive giantess, Madarque's sister, Andandona, a great enemy of Christians and eventually killed by Gandalín (in Chapter 68). Book III also introduces the evil King Arábigo, Arcaláus's ally and enemy of Lisuarte and Amadís until the end. The book closes with the arrival of Queen Sardamira of Sardinia and of Salustanquidio, El Patín's emissaries come to take Oriana to Rome. An unnamed damsel intercedes with King Lisuarte to try to dissuade him from the Roman marriage and she is given a hearing (in Chapter 80), while the same chapter provides another interesting social insight with the reappearance of Amadís's dwarf Ardián, who, delighted, is made "maestresala" or chief servant and taster, at the feast on the Ínsola Firme, and who also acts as a comic entertainer.

Book IV carries on with the social coverage by gathering many characters together for the great battles, and by making use of the Ínsola Firme and also of Gaul as bases of attack and defense against Lisuarte and El Patín. We recall too the treacherous campaign mounted by Arcaláus and Arábigo. The role of Nasciano as peacemaker need only be mentioned again. Here too we find the great concourse of kings, queens, princes, and princesses, and many knights and ladies and their attendants on the Ínsola Firme following the reconciliations and the marriages. The new characters appear in the adventure of the Queen of Dacia, whom Bruneo, Angriote, and Bruneo's brother Branfil help against the usurping Duke of Sweden, and in the subsequent adventures up to the end of Book IV. Thus Darioleta, formerly the damsel of Queen Elisena, Amadís's mother, reappears as widow of the governor of Little Britain, and Amadís defeats on her behalf the giant Balán, who, however, becomes his friend. (Balán, in a manner typical of the romance, we are told, was son of the giant encountered earlier, Madanfabul, who was defeated by Amadís, and of another Madasima, aunt of the giantess of the same name who married Galvanes.) A further adventure is provided by King Trafinor's son and Melicia's husband, Grasandor, who goes in search of Amadís and who also joins the brothers Eliseo and Landín in fighting the tyrannical Galifón. Arcaláus's wife too appears and proves again to be as good as her husband is evil—and for her Amadís fulfills a vow (in Chapter 130) taken early on.

Book IV also contains several brief references to the "gente más baxa," or the lower orders, and to their reactions. (There are many such frank class identifications in medieval literature). Thus (in Chapter 83) they show great joy and give shouts at Oriana's decision to go to the Ínsola Firme, while again (in Chapter 105) they show special joy and spirit at the news of the help for Amadís promised by the emperor of Constantinople; they are also seen displaying fear at the outcome of Quadrangante's proposal that Amadís seek allies against Lisuarte and El Patín (in Chapter 85). Once more their position and duties relative to those of their betters are clearly set out, when (in Chapter 84) they are housed on the Ínsola Firme with their masters but in keeping with their lowly rank, and when (in Chapter 95) Durín, brother of the Damsel of Denmark and an important messenger in the *Amadís*, avers that "las otras personas más baxas" also experience different anguish and cares from those which afflict rulers and the great in general. Finally (in Chapter 122), this very general category of humble people is referred to as being easily defeated in battle (in the adventure of Angriote, Branfil, and Bruneo on behalf of the Queen of Dacia), "como fuessen gente de baxa manera" ("as people of low kind").

When peace has been restored, festivities are held on the Ínsola Firme and these include (in Chapter 120) "trasechadores," or jugglers and acrobats, who, after dinner, entertain Amadís and others at King Perión's dwelling, with many games, until bedtime. Later (in Chapter 129), Grasandor, in his search for Amadís, meets "vn monje, de los blancos" ("a white friar"), and, as he worships in his little monastery asking God's help for his journey, he is told he is in a lordship of Ireland at present subjugated by the tyrant Galifón. Thus again we have an example of the role of the religious and of a minor character type who plays the important role of informant. The frequent appearance of monks in the countryside provides another authentic feature of the background to medieval life as portrayed in the romance.

A secondary but curious feature of the *Amadís* is the use of nicknames for some of its characters, although this too (as has been shown by Miss Williams and others) has plenty of precedents and parallels in the Arthurian literary corpus. We can omit from this category of names the many which identify characters by their country or place of origin, since, although even these do testify to the variety of the work, they are not strictly nicknames. Our hero, it will be recalled, rejoices in no fewer than six. He was abandoned to the sea with the sobriquet "Sin Tiempo" ("Without Time," since it was not thought he would survive); after his rescue fom the sea and his rearing by Gandales, he was appropriately known as the "Doncel del Mar" ("Youth of the Sea"), while in succession, and as a recognition of his deeds and attachments, he comes to be known as the "Caballero del Enano" ("The Knight of the Dwarf"), the "Caballero de la Verde Espada" ("The Knight of the Green Sword"), and the "Caballero Griego" ("The Greek Knight"). Also, during Amadís's exile on the Peña Pobre and for some time after, he uses the name "Beltenebrós," given to him by the hermit Andalod, who explained that it indicated both his handsome youthfulness and the grief of his mind.

The good fairy is, as we know, called Urganda la Desconocida, because no one knows exactly who she is; her magical powers (she

appears as both a maiden and an old woman) are set beside her
wisdom and power of prophecy, and thus she declares to Galaor on
one occasion (in Chapter 59) that her name is Sabencia Sobresaben-
cia (Knowledge More than Knowledge). Her evil counterpart Arcaláus is known as El Encantador (The Enchanter), since in this way
he abuses his power. Amadís's son and heir, Esplandián, is, toward
the end (in Chapter 126), given by Urganda the name "Caballero de
la Gran Serpiente" ("Knight of the Great Serpent"), to symbolize his
association and dependence upon her beneficent creature which
will bring him aid and succor on many occasions. Other, minor,
characters with whom either Amadís or Lisuarte have contacts,
include Galvanes sin Tierra (Galvanes without Land, since he only
has a castle), Ardán Canileo el Dudado (so called because of his
uncertain nature), Dardán el Soberbio (Haughty), whom Amadís
early defeats, Guilán el Cuidador ("the one who cares"), and Gasquilán el Follón (the Lazy or Negligent), the son of the giant
Madarque and later king of Suesa. There are also several more
characters who carry nicknames and who appear once or only a few
times, and are known as El Bravo (the Wild), El Valiente (the
Valiant), or El Orgulloso (the Proud), while one is known as El
Esgremidor (the Fencer), another as El Embidioso (the Envious),
another as El Lozano (the Lusty).

This practice is applied to only a few main characters and then to a
handful of lesser figures. It adds a certain flavor to someone whose
conduct or character is thus isolated and identified, and the symbolism of the romance is likewise increased, but in other cases it has
little illustrative value. Nicknames, as we know, also serve Amadís
as disguises, both at Lisuarte's court and abroad in eastern Europe,
and we shall look later at the importance of symbols in the novel.
The nickname is applied exclusively to certain principal characters
and to some other knights. The patchiness of its application would
suggest that this survival from the older romances was of limited
appeal to the author or authors of the Amadís.

The convincing picture of society that emerges from the Amadís is
yet another facet of the variety of its contents, and the multiplicity of
characters introduced appear as recognizable types from the older
European dispensation. They also further illustrate the values and
aims of the romance, which we have already seen made explicit in
the author's prologues and comments. It is also worth pointing out
here that the social hierarchy of the Amadís will be seen to fit

naturally into the general background and the geography of the novel, to be examined below. There emerges a clearly aristocratic and rural society (cities play only a small role), in which the order of things and classes is unquestioned and remains stable despite the stresses and strains imposed on it, as we have seen, by some of its most eminent members. This contrasts significantly with the restless and more vulnerable society and institutions which form the background of a lot of later fiction and drama, often themselves placed in an urban setting. The older romance, with the *Amadís* as one of its chief representatives, moves in an essentially changeless world of ultimate optimism and thus recalls that of the literary epic derived from Virgil and much cultivated during the 1500s and 1600s. In both genres the hero is submitted to tests and trials but he and his professed ideals come out at the end triumphant and unchallenged. This can be said to present an idealized vision of the world. On the other hand, European society weathered many changes before it met with truly revolutionary threats to its stability, and these came in the 1600s and 1700s, that is, much later in time than the society that produced the *Amadís* and that which it reflects.

II *Values and Habits*

More than one reference has been made to the moral values, or lack of them, and the psychological motives which explain the decisions and the conduct of the characters, and it is hardly necessary to go through the long book in search of details of what is self-evident to the attentive reader. Some general statement, however, on this important aspect of the *Amadís* will not come amiss at this point. The role of love will be dealt with separately as a major theme in the romance.

The *Amadís* is most clearly a work of fiction which exalts the order of knighthood and the institution of the monarchy. This is amply demonstrated in Chapters 31 and 32 of Book I, which give a striking account of Lisuarte's assembly in London, whither have come knights and ladies from many places and lands. Not only does Lisuarte acknowledge how his honor is increased by their presence, but he will through them seek to attract even more dedicated knights to his court. He wishes to be liberal and to reward his knights as Alexander, Julius Ceasar, and Hannibal did, since riches, he says, are not for hoarding. Further, the queen herself asks for and receives a pledge from them all that in addition they should fulfill their duty to protect ladies and damsels as the weaker sex, so that these may thus be safe upon the roads of the kingdom from the attacks and insults of insolent and violent men. In this way the *cortes* took a decision to reaffirm and apply anew the precepts of chivalry, and we are told that Great Britain for long afterward kept to them. We have also seen how Amadís went from the assembly to fulfill his vow to Briolanja.[3]

As previously observed there are many cases of how Amadís and other knights put these rules into practice against the enemies of Lisuarte, such as Arcaláus and the evil giants and other challengers who crop up throughout the book. We come across the many exchanges which precede battles and often include reminders by the knights to their antagonists of the right and wrong of the dispute in question. Often, too, battle is preceded by the hearing of mass (the role of religion is also to be examined separately below). In some cases, also, a concomitant of this dedication to justice, strengthened by religion, is the harsh and summary execution of a sentence on the evildoer. For example, Galaor (in Chapter 12) orders an evil dwarf to be tortured, although this same creature orders similar treatment to be meted out to a damsel; Lisuarte orders the usurper Barsinán and Arcaláus's cousin to be burned alive (in Chapter 38); Amadís (in Chapter 61) cuts off the tyrant Ardán's head and throws his body into the sea; in Chapter 75 Bruneo's squire appears with the severed heads of two knights killed by Angriote; and the Queen of Dacia (in Chapter 122) has the Duke of Sweden executed according to the full rigor of the law. Equally, there are quite a few cases (some have already been seen) of justice tempered by mercy: for example, Lisuarte orders surgeons to cure and heal his opponents (in Chapter 67); Esplandián successfully pleads with Amadís for two Romans (in Chapter 79); Briolanja spares the life of her treacherous cousin Trión (in Chapter 97); Amadís spares those of Arábigo's soldiers at Lubaina (in Chapter 117); and Galifón's full confession of crimes wins him pardon from Landín (in Chapter 129). Thus again characters are seen to be drawn not alone as cardboard figures of good and bad, but also with sharp and recognizable human traits.

Over all the actions of the many characters in the *Amadís* we find universal and unquestioned acceptance of the two pillars of an older society, namely, the monarchy and the church. Hence we have seen the strongest criticism leveled against both those who usurp or subvert the former and those who ignore or forget the teachings of the latter. It is a stable society, as stated before, despite the threats it receives. Indeed, it could be said that the *Amadís* is in great part about this, that is, a fictional study of the monarchy and of how, under God and with man's help, it survives as head of the natural order. Amadís is born a prince and eventually becomes a king, as does his son.

The riches of our romance can be further grasped if we look in some more detail at the conduct and life-style of the characters in their world.

First, and again in addition to those cases already noted, the subject matter of the *Amadís* often introduces us to humdrum human acts and situations, thus adding credence to the atmosphere of heroics and superhuman deeds that tend to prevail (the realism to be found in our romance will be dealt with separately below as part of the coverage of background and description). As a rather unexpected relief to the continuous encounters and combats comes the little detail of the knight guarding a bridge (in Chapter 17) while playing draughts with another; this he gives up as Amadís approaches and is challenged. Another sidelight on knightly conduct is provided by Galaor (in Chapter 23), who, after killing his opponent, goes to sleep on his helmet and covers himself with his shield, while later Amadís's faithful squire falls asleep after being awake for two days and nights (in Chapter 48). More dramatically, Amadís, finding himself unarmed and overpowered by others (in Chapter 33), is so chagrined that blood runs from his nose and eyes, while (again in Chapter 48) his dwarf Ardián bangs his head against a wall through grief for his master.

Details of a more domestic or day-to-day nature also occur: Oriana, for the writing of her calamitous letter to Amadís (in Chapter 44), uses ink and parchment; Amadís's tired horse is allowed to graze on green branches (in Chapter 46); Oriana is portrayed as sitting in a window reading a book (in Chapter 53), that is, before Amadís returns, while later (in the same chapter) she throws Mabilia on the floor and romps with her for joy; then later again (in Chapter 55) Leonoreta and her damsels and young girls make garlands of flowers for their heads to celebrate their deliverance from the giants by Amadís; and we come across another game when Gandalín discovers Amadís and Oriana playing chess at Miraflores (in Chapter 56).

There are several accounts of the collection of the dead and their burial after a battle as well as the curing of the wounded. A curious example of this last concerns the wounded Galaor (in Chapter 59), attended by two damsels who read to him from books of history (or fiction?) and who keep him awake during the day. References to hunting also enliven the scene: Lisuarte is described as much given to the chase, even to the detriment of his duties (in Chapter 23); merlins are used by the king (in Chapter 62), while he and his family take tents and other necessities when they set out to hunt (in Chapter 65); and, again, Lisuarte is greatly pleased when presented with two large deer (in Chapter 71). A more somber note, and one mixing realism and fantasy, is struck when the emissaries of the emperor of Constantinople are given perfumed boxes to cover their noses against the poison coming from the dead Endriago (in Chapter 74).

There are, of course, many references to the chivalric code; this is after all the main subject of the romance. This, indeed, softens the harshness of the final battles (in Chapter 104), when Galvanes asks Lisuarte not to compel him to fight against Amadís and Agrajes. Some other examples of chivalric practice are the holding of a pass by three knights (in the manner of the *Passo honroso*), in Chapter 43, the leaving of gages (a mantle and a silver hairnet) by Bruneo and the damsel against the battle of Ardán Canileo and Amadís (in Chapter 61), and, as a small example of the ritual of chivalry, the placing of a lance outside a tent, which we are told constitutes an invitation to joust (in Chapter 76). Brián de Monjaste is held (in Chapter 86) as beloved of all his companions, because of his continuous gaiety and playfulness, which are the marks of a man of good breeding.

So many references occur to eating and drinking that selection is very difficult. Still, there is the typical detail of the knight Brandoibas leading the lady Grindalaya by the hand and entering Lisuarte's palace at the time that the king's table was about to be laid (in Chapter 20). We can also recall the rather idyllic account of the alfresco meal enjoyed by Amadís and Oriana (after consummating their love) and by their attendants (in Chapter 35), a scene which anticipates many such in later fiction. There is too the ship which was sent out by Lisuarte to Rome under his nephew Giontes (in Chapter 104), which is well supplied with food as well as a crew. There are other cases of animals coming into the story: thus Queen Briolanja, on her way home, is accompanied by five horsemen and by three richly accoutered palfreys led by the reins (in Chapter 42);

also, Bruneo and his companions will only accept as gifts from the Queen of Dacia the hounds for which the region is famous (in Chapter 42); or we see how Amadís and Grasandor go out for relaxation to the hunt, with their helpers and hounds, where they expect to find wolves, boars, and other game (in Chapter 127). Perhaps a fitting detail with which to end this survey of the crudities and gentilities of medieval life in the *Amadís* is that which concerns Arcaláus: while in prison (in Chapter 130) he is given a book "of good examples and doctrines" (these very words, it will be recalled, were employed by Montalvo in his first prologue) to be used against the adversities of fortune.

Humor is a topic on its own in any account of human behavior, since it touches on many activities. Let us see a few cases from the *Amadís*, a book usually thought of as straight-faced, even solemn. It normally takes the form of references to laughter and is thus part of the account of how characters react. Seldom if ever can it be said that the author writes humorously, although it could also be held that to use it at all is in a way to write with humor. Further, laughter in the *Amadís* is for the most part divided into two categories. In the first, that which concerns a situation seen to be ridiculous or grotesque (and humor or the ridiculous was associated with the misshapen or the outrageous), we have, for example, the assembled company laughing at Amadís's dwarf, who speaks in fear of Arcaláus (in Chapter 19) because the latter had hung him up by the leg, while much later (in Chapter 69), Ardián again amuses Lisuarte as he scorns his tormentor whose palace is burning down, also to everyone's amusement. Lisuarte too is amused to hear how Guilán el Ciudador ("the lover who cares") is thrown off his horse by another (in Chapter 36) because he is lost in thought for his beloved (it is worth noting that this was often the state of mind of the lovelorn Amadís and as such it was treated seriously). Later King Cildadán expresses an old, macabre, even cruel humor as he laughs at the arrows sticking into the hide of the giantess Andandona as she flees (in Chapter 65). King Perión and others, on arrival at the Ínsola Firme, laugh at the account of how Arcaláus had in a cowardly fashion escaped capture by posing as Grumedán's cousin (in Chapter 69). This is yet another joke at the expense of the evil enchanter, as if the author wished to minimize the effects of his evildoing, by using humor as a kind of propitiation. Oriana and her ladies, as they are being unwillingly led to the Romans (in Chapter 80), experience her retinue's laughing scorn for the messenger of Agrajes and Florestán, namely, Guarte, who wishes to address her, but they also witness the turning of the tables on the retinue as Guarte makes Lasanor flee, and this provides them with much laughter. Much later (in Chapter 97), Oriana, Briolanja, and others laugh as they listen to Grasinda's account of Amadís's adventures and at how he humbles the knight Bradansidel by making him ride horseback turned around and holding the animal's tail, and, finally (in Chapter 125), a general reaction of this kind is expressed by those ignorant of the dangers involved in the tests on the Ínsola Firme, when they laugh at the discomfort of Amadís's sister Melicia, who gets only so far in the trial. Thus the traditional European sense of the ridiculous is made to inform quite a few incidents in our romance of adventures, and this normally reflects a robust pleasure at another's misfortune or mishap; sometimes, as with Arcaláus, the reader will be in full sympathy.

The other kind of humor, which is also the more common variety, denotes joy and pleasure and is usually an accompaniment of conversation or of activities and festivities at court or at the hunt. Also it often takes the form of verbal repartee. For example, Oriana laughs with pleasure (in Chapter 53) as Gandalín tells her to look after her appearance for Amadís's return; later (in Chapter 59), she and Briolanja and other ladies joke and laugh at Amadís's and Beltenebrós's "separate" skills in the Lovers' Arch and with the Burning Sword; Queen Brisena and Urganda (in Chapter 64) also laugh over the "deadly" charms of Oriana and Briolanja; much later (in Chapter 93), Oriana and the gay Brián de Monjaste and her ladies laugh at his wit, and Brián and his companions (in Chapter 97) laugh through joy with Amadís and his men as they arrive on the Ínsola Firme with Briolanja. There are less lighthearted examples: Dragonís, in the trial of the Burning Sword (in Chapter 57), chides Macandón, to everyone's delight, on his age and their respective ability to draw forth the sword; Queen Madasima and her ladies laugh at Amadís as he bests his fierce rival Ardán Canileo in a dispute (in Chapter 61); in Chapter 117, King Cildadán laughs at Amadís's attitude to the proud Gasquilán as he plays humble; and earlier (in Chapter 74) the emperor of Constantinople had laughed at Amadís's wit and pleasantries with his daughter and her ladies. Some cases involve Lisuarte and have a boisterous flavor: he jokes and laughs with King Cildadán and Galaor (in Chapter 66), saying he will not share his bag in their hunt, while later (in Chapter 71), Lisuarte laughs with Galaor and others when they bring him two large dead stags (in an episode we have seen before). Finally, a slightly different case, recalling perhaps the groups of ladies mentioned above, concerns King Perión as he talks and laughs with those accompanying him by ship to Gaul (in Chapter 69).

As with other material in the *Amadís*, humor forms a seasoning to the narrative. Although the cases occur as subordinate details of the main activities, they do help to fill in the picture that emerges, and they endow the characters with an added human quality.

III   *The Importance of Love*

The characters, many of whom are little more than types and remain rather shadowy, reveal themselves in more depth in an area of great significance in our romance, namely, love.

First, the *Amadís* can be regarded as a narrative which concerns itself chiefly with love and chivalric combat, and several critics, such as Menéndez y Pelayo, Miss Williams, Rodrigues Lapa, Miss Ruiz de Conde, and Mottola, have all examined in particular the nature and extent of the passion of Amadís and Oriana. It is recognized that this passion is both physical and idealized and that it differs from the adulterous love of, say, Lancelot and Guinevere, and from that of many courtly lovers, because of both its purity and its triumphant success. Let us look first at how this main thread of the novel's intricate plot develops. We shall also briefly consider some of the other manifestations of love in the *Amadís*, which tend to bring very much into relief the truly exceptional case of Amadís and Oriana as the prototypes of true love.

The love affair of Perión and Elisena, Amadís's parents, can be seen as a prelude or brief prefiguration of that of our hero and heroine (and, as has been seen by others, of several significant "parellels" in the story). It will be recalled that Perión and Elisena fell in love deeply and irrevocably in Chapter I, through the mutual attraction of physical beauty and moral reputation—Elisena for her sanctity and Perión for his deeds as a knight—and that they consummated their love almost at once. This was preceded by Perión's swearing on the hilt (or cross) of his sword to take her as his wife and is followed by vows of fidelity of which Perión's sword and ring were symbols, but his departure and Elisena's pregnancy meant that their son was born secretly and dispatched in a chest or

ark on the open sea. The reason for this secrecy was that all women
caught in extramarital love were then killed. This custom was
known as the law of Scotland and is also mentioned, for example, by
Ariosto (Montalvo's younger contemporary) in his *Orlando furioso*
(Canto IV). We are now told that it lasted for a long time until it was
eventually revoked by King Arthur himself. It is also clearly stated
that Elisena regarded herself as guiltless before God, if not before
the world, because their vows were secret. Soon afterward (in
Chapter 3) both lovers marry, although Perión had not yet heard of
his son. This case of true love also illustrates the old European
practice of secret marraige, studied, it will be recalled, for the early
Spanish romances, in the monograph by Josefina Ruiz de Conde.
Such alliances were regarded as binding, although they were often
made public by subsequent solemnization.

Amadís and Oriana, of course, also fall in love completely and
almost at first sign (in Chapter 4), when Oriana asks King Perión to
knight his own son. At this point we are told that in their case, as
with many lovers, the words used are few and simple and that the
author does not therefore try to state it otherwise. This constant
passion, which is to dominate the entire romance, is, however, told
at much greater length and its main features at least should be given
some analysis.

The traumatic and immediate effects of Amadís's absence from
Oriana are reminiscent of the reactions of Lancelot when away from
Guinevere, and this experience is repeated quite often in the
Amadís. Again, however, it is hardly necessary to say that we are far
from the adulterous relationships of the earlier hero and heroine.
Amadís displays some of the symptoms recorded by Ovid and the
courtly love tradition, namely, the abstraction of the lover from his
immediate surroundings or his great perturbation as he hears his
beloved's name or even calls her to mind. Thus (already in Chapter
5) he does not sleep for thinking of Oriana, while next day, as we are
graphically told, he is unaware of things as he crosses a bridge and a
little later almost falls from his horse as he hears a damsel pronounce
her name. He has a similar experience when (in Chapter 9) he
receives a letter from Oriana: the letter falls from his hand and he
lets go his rein, while once more (in Chapter 13) thoughts of her
bring tears to his eyes and cause him to lose consciousness. These
lover's upsets, brought about as they are by separation, are temporarily replaced by their opposite, unspeakable joy, when Amadís
is reunited with Oriana (in Chapter 14), and when she seems to him

to be the most beautiful woman on earth (the author here describes her in conventional terms as dressed in silk adorned with heavily gilded flowers and with a rich garland on her loose hair).

When (in Chapter 20) Arcaláus reports to Lisuarte's court that Amadís is dead, Oriana's grief is so great that she falls down as if dead. At their subsequent reunion (in Chapter 30) their joy is doubled, with Amadís's heart jumping from one side to the other, as the text vividly puts it, and an inability to utter a word or weep tears, and then the longest conversation so far in which they passionately express their feelings and fears. During all this early period and for long afterward they both keep their love secret (this narrative device and its opposite, discovery, have been examined above). Then, after Amadís is once more a prisoner and declares to his captor that he prefers death to disloyalty to Oriana (in Chapter 33), he proceeds to free her from Arcaláus's clutches and they thereupon consummate their love in idyllic conditions and follow it with the open-air repast referred to above (in Chapter 35). This climax is more explicitly a case of secret marriage (it had been recognized as such as early as Menéndez y Pelayo, who also refers to the tradition of the practice and the church's attitude). Amadís urges Oriana to comply and she grants his desire but with this significant phrase: "Yo haré lo que queréys y vos hazed cómo, avnque aquí yerro y pecado parezca, no lo sea ante Dios" ("I will do what you wish, and you act so that, although it may appear an error and a sin, it may not be so before God").

This, as we know, is to be followed by many griefs and two long separations before the lovers are finally reunited, and some of these episodes will be alluded to below, as they have been above. This is the place, however, to trace briefly the subsequent reaffirmation of their secret vows. Thus (in Chapter 71) the meeting of Oriana and Nasciano, when she confesses her love for Amadís and her parentage of Esplandián: in answer to the hermit's reproofs she asserts that, when they consummated their love, she had from him "palabra como de marido se podía y deuía alcançar" ("the word one could and should receive from a husband"). Nasciano is very pleased with this declaration (which, we are now told, will save many people, as will be seen in Book IV), and he absolves her. Much later (in Chapter 113), Nasciano in fact uses their secret union to persuade Lisuarte to seek peace, when, in answer to the latter's query as to whether Amadís and Oriana are married, he states: "Por cierto, verdad es . . . que él es maridò de vuestra hija, y el donzel Esplandián es

vuestro nieto" ("For sure, it is true . . . that he is your daughter's
husband, and the boy Esplandián is your grandson"). We can also
recall here how the author a little before this reflects on the power of
love (in Chapter 111). On his return from eastern Europe, Amadís
renews his vows to Oriana (in Chapter 103), and Amadís and Oriana
are, of course, finally recognized by Lisuarte as married and as his
heirs (in Chapter 118), thus making their relationship known to all.
Their passion is one of the great examples in literature and was as
such often proclaimed. Its depth of portrayal makes it still have an
appeal for us today, and its progress from secret vows to full public
avowal, with its human ups and downs, also places it in the category
of romantic love which overcomes all obstacles.

Perhaps the long and varied love affair of Amadís and Oriana may
be rounded off with some furthur reference to some of its main
characteristics. First, as Rodrigues Lapa pointed out, their passion
is portrayed as sensual and uplifting at the same time. Descriptions
of lovemaking (and those of other characters) follow the common
medieval pattern of using formulae. Thus, when Amadís and Oriana
consummate their love, the author's comment is: "On that grass and
top of that mantle, more by the grace and restraint of Oriana, than
by the forwardness or daring of Amadís, the most beautiful damsel
in the world was made a woman" (I, 285). On the other hand, we do
get closer to the reality of the experience (in Chapter 56), when
Amadís returns to Oriana at Miraflores after the period in Peña
Pobre. This scene of great erotic ecstasy is evoked in terms of the
traditional bower of bliss (of which the Ínsola Firme can be said to
be the recurring example in the *Amadís*), and it too is couched in
rhetorical terms to suggest its uniqueness; there is nevertheless
this realistic touch: "But who would be capable of telling of the
loving embraces, the sweet kisses, the tears which there were
mixed together mouth to mouth?" (III, 467).

The very special nature of this alliance can perhaps be most
dramatically exemplified by the reactions of Amadís to Oriana's
jealous letter, which causes him to go into the wilderness and
temporarily to become a hermit. This, as we know, is itself caused
by the passion of Queen Briolanja for Amadís, which, however, he
does not share. We here reach, rather early in the romance, it is
true, the real emotional and psychological climax (in Chapter 45),
the results of which, as we also know, help to shape the events of the
rest of the story. Amadís's grief is envisaged again in traditional

terms and with its own realism: he has now "arrived at cruel death, with so many tears, so many sighs, that it only seemed that his heart was broken in pieces, since he was in such a faint and as unconscious as if his soul had parted from his flesh" (II, 373). He bursts out into the stricken soliloquies referred to above, and decides to keep it all to himself and withdraw from the world. Setting off, he lets his horse lead him where it will and then he falls exhausted. We once more recall how such physical collapse and traumatic emotional crises afflicted Amadís's prototype from the older romances. Soon after, the wretched and unloved Amadís has to fight El Patín, his rival for Oriana's love (in Chapter 46). Amadís's departure for the wilderness is preceded by his frightening dream (in Chapter 48), but his agony reaches a new peak when, as a hermit (in Chapter 51), his physical state becomes critical, such is his unspeakable grief at the loss of Oriana's affection: "his health had reached such a state that he did not expect to live for two weeks more, and, because of his great weeping and his great weakness, his face was very thin and black, much more than if he had been suffering from a great illness" (II, 422).

Again attention should be drawn to the effects of grief, namely, lachrymosity and physical weakness, both typical of the Ovidian tradition of love which inspired literature up to the 1600s and after, and into the period of the romantic novel.[4] Indeed, this long account of Amadís's collapse under grief can be said to have several literary antecedents—and one should also recall here his little *canción* written at the height of his despair and translated in Chapter 4. This is, of course, not to say that the picture is lacking in psychological truth.

Not all their affair follows this pattern, since, soon after their reunion, both are proclaimed the perfect lovers when (in Chapter 57) they win the sword and the garland at Lisuarte's court, although they still hide their identity. We also recall here the great success of Amadís in the Ínsola Firme where (in Chapter 44) he becomes its lord because he succeeds in all the tests and passes under the Loyal Lovers' Arch. This island, it will be remembered, is to become the haven of Amadís and Oriana and others in Book IV. Once more, the later part of the romance records the continuing grief of the two lovers through separation. In Gaul, Amadís suffers the frustration of inactivity as a knight because of Oriana, and this is contrasted with the happiness of his loyal friend Bruneo and his beloved Melicia,

Amadís's sister (in Chapter 68). During his five years of exile and adventures in eastern Europe, the same is the case: the longing for the absent Oriana almost unbalances him and makes him forget his service to King Trafinor (in Chapter 70); he cannot put his beloved out of his mind even amid perils (in Chapter 72), and particularly so when he faces his greatest danger and challenge in fighting the fearsome Endriago (in Chapter 73), since at this perilous stage he commends himself almost as solemnly to his beloved as to his maker.

We can see how this episode has come to stand as a true symbol of all that Amadís strives for, since it touches not alone on his commitment to chivalry and love but also on his religious faith, as we shall point out again below. Even the splendor and the hospitality of the great court at Constantinople serve only to remind him of the absent Oriana, and we find him weeping publicly more than once and falling into a trance (in Chapter 74), although once again secrecy is preserved. Indeed his return home, after having made the reluctant commitment to bring the beautiful Grasinda back to Lisuarte's court, is motivated by the burning desire to be with Oriana (in Chapter 75).

There are many other incidents involving Amadís and Oriana as lovers, especially those which form an integral part of the long-drawn-out struggle with Lisuarte and El Patín as well as the final reconciliation. These, however, have been examined under another heading, although it should be noted here that they powerfully illustrate the persistence of this great love as it illumines the plot and contributes as a central topic to its fulfillment. The marriage of both lovers and of the other couples (arranged in Chapter 120) are solemnized by Nasciano (in Chapter 125) on the Ínsola Firme, where finally Oriana wins the lovers' tests against Melicia and Olinda and Apolidón's magic is declared ended when both Amadís and his beloved supersede the latter and Grimanesa as perfect lovers (also in Chapter 125). One of the last authorial comments in the romance (already quoted above) ends thus: "But let us cease speaking about the affairs of these loyal lovers, both because they keep going on, as also because very long years have passed by and will pass by before other such lovers may be seen or be remembered in writings of such length" (IV, 1286).

As stated above, and as any reader knows, the *Amadís* deals with many love affairs involving a whole range of characters. Of these perhaps those of Amadís's brother Galaor deserve some special mention, if only because they stand in such contrast to the distinctly monogamic dedication of our hero and thus in their way add to the latter's uniqueness as a lover.

First, the young Galaor, after defeating the giant Albadán who had taken the Peña de Galtares from the good giant Gandalás who himself had reared Galaor, is led by a damsel (in Chapter 12) to the castle of Grindalaya's sister, the beautiful Princess Aldeva, who receives him in the luxury of her bedchamber and then spends the night with him. The damsel significantly comments that since they are both of royal blood, "si vos mucho amáys, no vos lo terná ninguno a mal" ("if you love each other much, no one will take it ill"). The author, while using the usual kind of formula, is more explicit in describing this kind of union, and sets the tone for Galaor's casual affairs: "he dallied that night at his pleasure with the damsel; and no more need be said to you, since such acts, which are not in keeping with good conscience or virtue, should reasonably be passed over lightly and given the little importance which they deserve" (I, 105).

Later (in Chapter 25), as a result of and, it would seem, partly as a reward for avenging her father, the knight Antebón's murder by Palingues, Galaor is warmly welcomed by his grateful daughter Brandueta, who finds him both young and handsome. Then, as he speaks alone to her before the meal, and, as our text puts it wittily, mixing a standard evasive formula and a certain realism: "since she was very beautiful and he desirous of such a tidbit, before the meal came and the table was laid, both of them disarranged a bed which was in the castle where they were, he making a woman of her who was not one, and thus satisfying their desires, which in such a short space of time as they looked at each other in their flowering and beautiful youth had become very great" (I, 222). This frank account of sudden sexual passion and its satisfaction has about it a freshness that can be recalled in much early literature, notably, as indicated, in the *Tirant lo blanc*; it undoubtedly reflects contemporary court life. It also provides what one can call a normal dimension to the whole treatment of love in the *Amadís* by revealing the ordinary humanity of the hero's brother. Galaor and Brandueta soon after spend the night in bed together, since, as the author disarmingly says, she did not think it befitting his honor to leave him alone!

Not much later (in Chapter 33) Galaor finds a new companion in one of the three Madasimas in the *Amadís*, that is, the castellan of

Gantasi who has captured him and Amadís. Galaor found her very beautiful and very rich and a noblewoman, and she was more taken by him than by any other man, and so he lay ("yugo" is the Spanish term) with her for the night, thus, it seems, achieving both his and his brother's release! On the other hand, the same philanderer Galaor meets with a rebuff (in Chapter 41) when, searching for a knight (his half brother Florestán) with a beautiful damsel, she refuses to share her tent with him even though he too seems most attractive to her, and although he has a short time before said he would not then lie with her. Later again (in Chapter 69), Galaor, accompanied by Norandel (natural son of Lisuarte and the Princess Celinda, whom he has saved from the fierce Antifón and with whom he made love, in Chapter 66, underneath a rose tree), have an erotic adventure rather less acceptable to the reader perhaps than the other spontaneous affairs. This concerns Dinarda, daughter of Ardán Canileo and niece of Arcaláus, whom she had recently helped to imprison Amadís, his father, and others. Now she and her damsel, simply to preserve their lives, give themselves to the two knights without shame. Dinarda is here described as being most beautiful and dressed in red and white, while the author now also speaks of Galaor's "mañas" (or "habits") which lead him to want to have a beautiful woman.

Eventually Galaor, once his wild oats are sown, does fall truly in love with Queen Briolanja (now in the perfection of her beauty), whom he is to marry. The text is clear on the point: "although he has seen and had to do with many women, his heart had never been given in true love to any but this very beautiful queen" (IV, 1200). Briolanja on her side, we are told, is to give Galaor all the love she once had for Amadís. Thus we find Amadís's brother to the end portrayed as a very normal mortal in respect of the love for women. But then Amadís was in all he did a truly exceptional man.

The less exalted side of human love, as exemplified by Galaor, is brought within the general dispensation of reconciliation which marks the final winding up of much of the romance, and is significantly associated with the symbol of beneficence, Urganda la Desconocida. This concerns the result of a joint love affair of Galaor and Cildadán, King of Ireland, when (in Chapter 59) they were cured of their battle wounds by Urganda's two nieces, Julianda and Solisa (natural daughters, it is declared, of Lisuarte's brother, King Falangrís, and Urganda's sister, Grimota, when they were both young!) One of the nieces had earlier taken Amadís to Urganda (in Chapter 10) and he had subsequently saved her from violation by another knight (in Chapter 19). Galaor and Cildadán, in circumstances now familiar to us, left the two damsels pregnant and thus became the fathers of Talanque and Manelí el Mesurado (the Moderate). The future association of these two princes with Esplandián is referred to when kings and queens and many others finally gather on the Ínsola Firme (in Chapter 123). When, however, Talanque and Manelí have become youths, Urganda addresses both Galaor and Cildadán (in Chapter 126) and makes this interesting confession of responsibility for their births:

. . . it will be sufficient glory for me, since no lineage can be generated in my own person, that I should have been the cause of the births, in others, of such handsome youths as you see that I have here; for doubtlessly you may believe that they will perform such deeds that not only will those who fathered them against the commandment of Holy Church be pardoned, and I too who caused it, but their merits will be so increased that both in this world and afterward in the next they will win great rest, and I too will obtain even more. (IV, 1236)

This declared family relationship, both symbolic and literal, of Urganda with some of the protagonists, and in particular their descendants, on whom she places such high hopes, is now followed by her dedication to and special protection of Esplandián, to whom she commends her grandnephews as his helpers and close companions. Later again (in Chapter 133) there occurs, aboard Urganda's serpent-ship and in its chapel, where Esplandián and his several youthful companions had been brought, the impressive ceremony of the dressing of Esplandián in black armor by none other than Urganda's nieces and the mothers of Talanque and Manelí, namely, Solisa and Julianda. Vigil is then kept and further prayers are made before the Virgin's altar.

Urganda has acted as Amadís's good fairy from the beginning, and her supernatural arts have always been placed in the service of the upright and the chivalrous. She now also makes clear that she has close ties with humanity at its most basic level of collective living. It is of special significance that here, as with Amadís's own parents and those of Esplandián, not to mention Norandel's mentioned above, and the case of Florestán, son of King Perión and the daughter of the Count of Zeeland (in Chapter 42), extramarital relationships are tolerated and their results fully accepted. Several of the main figures of our romance on whose dedication so much of the action and meaning depends were either born out of wedlock—the secret marriage was, as we have seen, halfway between solemnization and no marriage at all—or themselves became the fathers of natural children. This tolerance for a sin of the flesh never regarded in an older European dispensation as the worst of the mortal sins undoubtedly reflects the social reality of the age, and, as such, can be seen in much medieval literature.

Side by side with this frank acceptance of casual or promiscuous sexual experiences, the *Amadís* also provides certain important examples of more conventional alliances. Thus the declarations of fidelity involving Agrajes and Olinda (in Chapter 23), Florestán and Corisanda (in Chapter 53), Galvanes and Madasima (in Chapter 62), and Bruneo and Melicia (in Chapter 65), all of whom are presented as cases of true love and thus recall even if faintly the great commitment of Amadís and Oriana. It is also worth pointing to the case of Amadís's friend Baláys de Carsante, who (in Chapter 28) makes a proposal of love to a damsel whom he has just rescued from thieves; when she rejects him Baláys apologizes and reaffirms the duty of knights to protect ladies and respect their virtue. Baláys (also in Chapter 28), it will be recalled, spent the night with two holy ladies. The reader will recall how the author a little later (at the end of Chapter 31) praises Amadís's other companion, Angriote de Estravaus, for respecting his beloved's chastity before their marriage (see our Chapter 4 above), and one will also recall the decision taken at the London assembly, and at the request of Queen Brisena (in Chapter 32), to protect ladies and damsels. A further final reference should be made to the multiple marriage ceremony (in Chapter 125) and to Amadís's and Oriana's idyllic life on the Ínsola Firme (in Chapter 127). If, as we know, these events do not end the action of the *Amadís*, at least they do constitute a very fitting conclusion to the careers of many of those who have made up our romance.

As one of the major experiences in human existence, love or the relationship between the sexes informs a very great deal of the art and literature of all ages and cultures. It is then hardly surprising that in the *Amadís* it provides a recurring note of realism and of common humanity, and that, as in the case with certain other aspects of the novel seen above, it presents characters of flesh and blood. Perhaps more than any of the other elements that go to make up our many-sided romance (some have been analyzed and some others will now also be examined), this one will readily awaken in the modern reader an interest in the fictional portrayal of a society and its values that have long since passed away. Fewer readers will now join Menéndez y Pelayo in stressing the *Amadís*'s fantasy at the expense of the repeated reflection in its pages, as with the topic of love, of life's basic truths and experiences.

The theme of love in our romance can be said to be presented on two levels. First, there is that of fidelity between lovers and on the basis of solemn vows, and second, that of temporary or fleeting attachments. These two types are not, however, completely different the one from the other, since the physical aspect of the passion is explicitly associated with both kinds. Thus the initial attractiveness of one person for the other or the actual reference to sexual union are commonplaces in the handling of the subject. This indeed can be said to have made the overwhelming and idealized passion of Amadís and Oriana more acceptable to readers of different periods. It is true, however, that the *Amadís*'s treatment of love recalls some medieval examples rather than others. First, it is generally presented as leading to happiness and fulfillment, whereas both the *Cárcel de amor* and the *Celestina* deal with frustrated and tragic cases of true love. The *Tirant lo blanc* forms a closer parallel, in so far as Tirant and Carmesina are also faithful lovers who have sexual relations before their union is solemnized, although this hero, ironically and unlike Amadís, does not live very long to enjoy his final happiness. On the other hand, the *Tirant* goes even further than the *Amadís* in describing lovemaking. Both novels also illustrate conjugal passion, which was often frowned upon by Christian moralists, and both present human love as something natural and its manifestations as readily tolerable. While the *Tirant* and the *Amadís* contain many passages written in the sophisticated and witty language typical of the sentimental novel and the love lyric of the period, both romances, as examples of triumphant love, do not greatly share the prevalent suicidal tone of these other genres of erotic literature. The *Tirant*, like the *Amadís*, can be said to deal rather more with courtly life than with courtly love.[5]

Having made these few comparisons and contrasts, it will perhaps not be thought inappropriate to state that in the *Amadís* love is presented as something relatively simple rather than complex and as having an optimistic outcome. It is therefore not surprising that our romance should have provided the material for one of early modern Europe's most popular manuals of court behavior. The *Amadís* thus reflects life as well as established literary conventions.[6]

IV   *The Role of Religion*

The characters of the *Amadís* also reveal themselves and the world to which they belong in their attitude to religion (this again has been referred to above). In his first prologue Montalvo tries to prepare us for the right reading and the emphasis to be given to his romance. Thus we are to learn and take example from feats of arms for the salvation of our souls. Indeed, he explicitly avers that the changes he made in the earlier *Amadís* include such "exemplos y doctrinas" which now accompany a tale that was originally regarded merely as "patrañas", or fiction. His prologue, it will be remembered, also ends on a pious note: "And if by chance there should appear in this badly ordered work one of those errors not allowed in the affairs of God or man, I humbly ask pardon for it, since, as I hold and believe firmly all that Holy Church holds and commands, the cause of it has been my simple wit rather than the work itself" (I, 10).

As soon as the reader enters upon the story he is told that its events took place not long after Our Lord and Redeemer's passion. But he also soon finds that the text offers one reference to religion after another. This, as we shall see, is to continue uninterruptedly until the very end.

Several critics as far back as Menéndez y Pelayo have commented upon the tone which it is held was given to the *Amadís* material by Montalvo. Some, like Olmedo and Gili y Gaya, have emphasized how, as the romance progresses, and especially in Book IV, both Amadís and Esplandián are presented more and more with a Christian emphasis. This is, of course, even more explicitly the case with Esplandián as the hero of Book V, or the *Sergas*. Thus it is now freely recognized (and Anthony Mottola recently did so) that, unlike its models and their later Spanish versions, the *Amadís* is in this respect a new kind of romance of chivalry. One systematic account of the role of religion in our romance is that provided by Mário Martins. This scholar points to the details of Amadís's upbringing, the exile on Peña Pobre, and repeated references to religion in the addresses by the author to the reader. Martins also refers to the many exclamations in the text and he observes how the knights move in a world in which time is measured in monastic terms (thus the references to vespers or matins or nones) or a date is attached to a religious feast. He also notes, as we too have seen above, that the protagonists frequently meet with hermits and regularly keep vigil, confess, and hear mass, and that this recurrence of piety forms part of a way of life which also commonly includes love and combat. Even this short analysis of the place of religion in the *Amadís* once more reveals the complex texture of the romance (for the article by Martins, see our bibliography).

It will be recalled that mention has been made in this monograph of the role, in Books III and IV, of such characters as the holy man Nasciano. There is also the intervention of Elisabad, both as priest and physician (in Chapter 73), for his role with Amadís in the defeat of the Endriago, when he sets up an altar with relics to say mass for Amadís's victory. This episode is explicitly conceived as a struggle between the devil and God (and in his body the monster unites the features of the three devils worshiped by its father); as a high point in our hero's career it has a significance which covers a range of different aspects, including chivalry and love (for Amadís, as we have seen, commends himself both to Oriana and to God). Much of what has been discussed above, for example the authorial comments and the section on love and marriage, is inseparably bound up with religious references, and thus at this point any extensive repetition is uncalled for.

Still, we should recall in passing that God's will is clearly seen in the London assembly (in Chapter 31), in His support of a just king like Lisuarte (in Chapter 35), in the Christian duty to fight a crusade like Ferdinand and Isabella (in Chapter 42), in His rearing of the scions of royal houses (in Chapter 71), in bringing about a final peace through Esplandián and Nasciano (in Chapters 111 and 113), and, of course, in the final marriages (in Chapter 125). The reader will thus be left in no doubt that the institution which dominates the *Amadís*, namely, the monarchy, is in God's hands: for example (in Chapter 74), the emperor of Constantinople is referred to as the "mayor hombre de los christianos" ("the greatest man of the Christians"), and his city as the head of Christendom (much as had been said of London in Chapter 31), while, in Chapter 95, Lisuarte calls himself God's lieutenant. The author in his comments, as we know, keeps referring to a king's duty under God and how all his acts, both public and private, are subject to His will.

The final speeches and acts of Urganda, as we have also noted, make very explicit the religious nature of Esplandián's dedication and his future career (in Chapters 126 and 133). Thus our long romance draws to its close with increasing significance being given to the religious aspects and implications of events. Brief passing mention should again be made of the enemies of the faith; thus, for example, the giantess Andandona (in Chapter 65) and, of course, the devil's own agent, the Endriago (in Chapter 73). The Christians on the Ínsola de la Torre Bermeja (in Chapter 128) are oppressed by pagan giants; other giants, however, helped to serve and protect the faith (see note 2 to this chapter).

Some further account should be given of the way in which religion or piety forms part of the very style of the *Amadís* from beginning to end, thus creating a distinctive and pervasive quality that is inseparable from the story this style clothes. For example, a simple count of the number of times any reference is made to religion or God or the Virgin, in Book I, reveals that there is at least one for each one of its three hundred fifty or so pages (that is, in the Place edition). Many of these references fall into the category mentioned, although very much in passing, by Martins, namely, exclamations or oaths which always seem to be on the lips of speakers. Thus, "por Dios" ("by God"), "por Sancta María" ("by Saint Mary"), "por Dios vos ruego" ("by God I beg you"), "si querrá Dios" ("if God will wish it"), "en el nombre de Dios" ("in the name of God"), "assí Dios vos vala" ("thus may God help you"), "bendito sea Dios" ("blessed be God"), "que Dios maldiga" ("may God curse"), "a Dios merced" ("to God grace"), "Dios queriendo" ("God willing"), "a Dios vayáis" ("may you go with God"), "Dios os dé honrra" ("may God give you honor"), "Dios os guarde de traición" ("may God keep you from treason"). Variations of these phrases also occur in profusion.

Another equally common and related variety of religious reference concerns a more deliberate act of remembrance, which also reveals an established pattern of life. Thus the taking of an oath on the host by three clerics so that they would honestly interpret King Perión's dream (in Chapter 2); or the very common practice of a knight commending himself to God or being commended by another (as Oriana does to her new lover Amadís, in Chapter 4), that is, as adventure or danger is undertaken, and the most elaborate and solemn example of this for Amadís is, of course, when he undertakes to fight the dread Endriago (in Chapter 73). There is also the very common practice of giving thanks or blessing to God for safety or deliverance or victory, as when (in Chapter 54) Oriana hears that Amadís is alive; the reader also notes that the sign of the cross is made to indicate wonder or fear, as when Queen Brisena finds the crown and the mantle missing from her chest, in Chapter 31 (this in fact is later revealed, in Chapter 34, to have been the work of the evil enchanter Arcaláus). God's providence is often remarked upon as when, in Chapter 52, the Damsel of Denmark arrives safely at the Peña Pobre from the fearful storm at sea, or when, in Chapter 70, Amadís expresses emphatically, to King Trafinor and others, his trust in God's guidance for his affairs. And God, as we have seen in the authorial comments (and many briefer examples of these can be found in the text) punishes the wicked and the sinful. These cases are also, of course, among the commonplace uses of religion, and can be encountered in many works of literature.

As for further examples of acts inspired by religious faith, mention can be made of the frequency with which in the *Amadís* the author refers to the characters hearing mass: thus, from among many such cases, Amadís, Galaor, and Balays, before they set out for Windsor, hear mass and then put on their armor (in Chapter 24); Galaor and King Cildadán, on their way to Lisuarte's court, and after spending the night in a forest, hear the mass bell and go to the nearby church (in Chapter 66); and, on a more solemn occasion, Nasciano prepares to say mass at the celebration of the marriages (in Chapter 125). This, the church's central sacrament, is a repeated accompaniment of the ordinary action of the book, namely, combat and adventure, and constitutes perhaps the most telling illustration of the role of religion in the *Amadís*.

In this world where knights often meet hermits (and we recall again that Amadís himself was at one time a hermit), there are also cases of confession: thus our hero, as he wanders in great distress at Oriana's angry letter, meets the religious Andalod and unburdens himself, is absolved, and receives his blessing (in Chapter 48), while again, before battle with Ardán Canileo, he awakens the chaplain, has him hear his confession, and then prays to the Virgin for her help (in Chapter 61). We find Oriana (in Chapter 117) praying a lot, and making pilgrimages to the churches on the Ínsola Firme, for peace and an end to the strife. There is also the isolated but interesting case of the thief who, prevented by Balays from violating a damsel, becomes a "hombre bueno de buena vida" ("a good man living a good life") and a hermit (in Chapter 28). More striking perhaps is Amadís's decision (in Chapter 45) to honor the Virgin, in whose hermitage he has prayed after receiving Oriana's letter, by founding there a monastery in her name for thirty friars, the cost to be met from the income of the Ínsola Firme. This in fact is done, and his savior and fellow hermit in the Peña Pobre, Andalod, carries out the task by appointing Sisián and thirty companions (in Chapter 63).

The constant reminders at the level of the most commonplace verbal utterances or of everyday actions and reactions of an unquestioned faith all point to an interpenetration of life and religion which can, of course, be observed in other areas of medieval culture. God and religion are seen to preside over all things and to be associated with man's every thought, but then one would expect this to be the case with a literary text of the period of Ferdinand and Isabella and one that reflects society even on a fictional plane.

CHAPTER 6

Magic, Symbol, and Dreams

IF the *Amadís* is permeated with references to religion and examples of religious practice, it can also be said that its action moves in a world which exists under the influence of magic or enchantment. This can be both good or bad, or white and black, that is, beneficent and evil in its effects, and, further, its positive manifestations can be regarded as an aspect of the supernatural. There can be no doubt that in this the *Amadís* has inherited material from the older Breton romances in which magic also played an important role. In these latter we also meet with material itself inherited from a pre-Christian past. Our romance, however, in this matter, as in the other topics it has taken from its chief sources, displays an original rearrangement of episodes and characters which reflect its own fresh view of chivalry and love. It is also worth mentioning at this point that the other main European body of romance, namely, the Carolingian, culminating in Ariosto's poem the *Orlando furioso*, likewise made considerable use of enchantment and indeed that it sometimes drew on the same sources.

Magic is chiefly associated with two important figures. First, there is Urganda la Desconocida, who recalls the Lady of the Lake from the Lancelot story, and other such figures from the Breton cycle. Urganda is the good fairy who presides over the destinies of Amadís, Esplandián, and others, and, as we have seen, who also developed a kind of family connection with some of the main protagonists. Second, there is Arcaláus el Encantador (Enchanter), the prototype of the enemy of all good, the devil figure of the romance, who, although he uses magic when in a tight corner, increasingly becomes the intriguer and organizer of opposition to Lisuarte and Amadís and thus acquires a very human appearance, especially when he is nearly burned to death in his castle or when he is finally imprisoned. Magic is also associated with the Ínsola Firme,

111

first introduced at the beginning of Book II, but this, however, is of
a distinct kind and takes the form of physical trials intended to test
the moral standing of the main characters; however, it shares with
the enchantment practiced by Arcaláus the upsetting of the natural
order of the physical world, whereas Urganda uses magic to impress
rather than to impede (on two occasions, however, in Chapters 60
and 133, she harmlessly and temporarily puts her friends to sleep).
There is in addition the magic associated with Esplandián's birth
letters.

I *Urganda la Desconocida*

Urganda appears throughout the *Amadís*, although more frequently in Books I and IV, whereas the magical events in the Ínsola
Firme belong to Book II for the most part, and the equivalent
activities of Arcaláus occur mostly in Book I. The last named (together with King Arábigo and others) plays a very important part in
the later struggles involving Amadís and Lisuarte in Books III and
IV, when, as stated, his role is that of a cunning and determined
warrior rather than that of a sorcerer. Although Urganda and Arcaláus do not meet and thus do not come into conflict either directly
or through their agents, the former certainly knows of the designs
and the actions of the latter, while Arcaláus has reason on one
occasion to curse Urganda in very unflattering terms. As will be
seen, one of Urganda's chief functions is that of prophetess and
moralizer, and thus it is natural that such an evildoer as Arcaláus
should come within her ken.

Urganda makes her first appearance in the strange adventure of
enchantment and combat with Gandales, another knight (whom she
declares to be her lover) and another damsel (in Chapter 2). She is
later involved with her lover (in Chapter 11), whom yet another
lady, not fearing Urganda's powers, holds in her castle, but she is
forced to free him through Amadís's superior skill in arms; Urganda
is to remember with deep gratitude this act of kindness and this will,
it seems, influence her sponsorship of our hero. Thus, our first sight
of this formidable enchantress is as a young girl in love—one recalls
at this point her much later statement that it was through her nieces
rather than herself that her succession was to come. However (also
in Chapter 2), she changes her appearance to that of an old woman,
who now prophesies to Gandales the great future of Amadís, his
ward. This fusion of two roles is not consistently maintained, al-

though she again appears as a girl (in Chapter 5) when she gives Amadís his lance and foresees his coming deeds. It is also stated at this point that she lives on her own island; the prevalence of this geographical feature in the *Amadís* will be commented upon later. This abode has the significant name of the Ínsola no Fallada (the "island that is not found," an echo of the appellation by which Urganda herself is generally known). Later (in Chapter 10) Urganda sends a damsel to remind King Perión of her prophecy (in Chapter 2) and of how he has won a son. (Here she also refers to the connection between Abiés of Ireland and Tristan, King Marc, and Isolt, this being one of the few specific mentions in our romance of the ancient Breton material.) At the same point in the story another damsel refers to her mistress Urganda as the one from whom affairs cannot escape, and Amadís speaks of her as the one whom people need. There is only one other intervention by Urganda in Book I and this again indirect, when (in Chapter 19) yet another damsel, who says she is her niece, is sent to save Amadís and others from the enchantments of Arcaláus.

In Book II (and in Chapter 57) there are read out Urganda's letters of warning to Lisuarte and Galaor (also referred to above). Here too Lisuarte is made to reconsider his plans by the awareness that Urganda was "so knowledgeable that for the most part all those things which she prophesied came true . . ." (II, 482). This view of Urganda's powers is repeated more than once before the end of the novel and is given more than once too as the reason for her great influence on events.

Urganda's next (indirect) intervention occurs when (in Chapter 58) she again sends a damsel, from the Ínsola no Fallada, bearing gifts, this time for Perión and his two sons, Amadís and Florestán. The girl comes richly dressed and on a very handsome palfrey, and accompanied by three squires and a nag which carries a bundle. The gifts are three shields, with golden serpents on a silver field worked on them and with golden borders of precious stones, three emblems similarly worked, and three helmets of different colors. These are to allow their users to recognize each other in battle. The damsel, who cannot tell how Urganda knew that the three knights were to take part in the coming encounter, does say that her mistress asks Amadís in particular to act better than he has been doing lately (that is, during his idle stay in Gaul). Very shortly afterward (in Chapter 59) we come across the love making between Urganda's two nieces

and Galaor and Cildadán, already examined above. All that need be
added is that Urganda knew what she was doing in arranging this
union and thus made herself known to the two knights and told
them how she had taken them by enchantment to save and cure
them. Thus once more she intervenes and here directs the course of
events, even influencing the final outcome of the romance, as we
have also seen.

Soon after this Urganda appears in a very new guise in which her
near normal appearance as a young or old woman is changed into
that of a *dueña* (lady), who now approaches by sea and is accompanied by magical forces that alarm and astonish her protégés. Thus,
in Chapter 60, in which she is referred to as "la Encantadora"
(Enchantress), her arrival takes place as Lisuarte and his court are
casually preparing for bed after supper. The event and its effect are
dramatically told:

The king saw two fires coming toward the town, at which all were
frightened, since it seemed strange to them that fire should accommodate
itself to water. But getting closer they saw coming between the fires a galley
on whose mast two great candles were burning so that the whole galley
seemed on fire. The noise was so great that everyone from the town went
out to the walls to see this wonder, expecting that, since the water could not
put out that fire, nothing else could do so and the town would be burned
down. (II, 511)

The townspeople were very afraid and the queen and her ladies
went to the chapel to pray, while Lisuarte and his knights, including
Amadís, took horse and approached the fire. Soon, however, there
emerged from beneath a cloth on the ship a lady dressed in white
with a little gold box in her hands. From this she took a lighted
candlestick which, when once it is thrown into the sea and put out,
the other fires also go out and disappear, the only remaining light
coming from the candles on the masthead which lit up the whole
beach. The cloth having then been taken from the ship, the latter
revealed itself covered in branches and flowers and from it came the
sweet sound of musical instruments. These ceased and out came ten
richly dressed damsels with garlands and carrying golden rods,
while the lady now stood before the king but still aboard the galley.
They all bowed to one another.

This theatrical entrance is clearly meant to impress those who saw it and also to demonstrate Urganda's power and reveal her presence clearly, and it is all in striking contrast to the almost evasive earlier appearances of the enchantress. It should also be noted that these different kinds of appearances correspond respectively to meetings with individuals and to assembled companies. In other words, what is effective for the private encounter is quite unsuitable for the public confrontation. Thus Urganda now declares herself openly and explains that all this use of fire is for the protection of herself and her damsels. After spending the night in a tent on the beach, she proceeds to warn the king about evil counselors, and then diplomatically praises the beauty of Oriana and Briolanja and speaks of the tests of the burning sword and the flowered headdress won by Amadís and Oriana (in Chapter 57). After assuring the latter that she will not reveal her secret, she reads in a tiny book and sends all the ladies into a deep sleep, that is, except for Oriana, to whom she also foretells, in a kind of parable involving a lion, her future unhappiness, which, however, will be tempered by the love of Amadís.

Finally, after a few days' rest at court, Urganda has Lisuarte bring the two letters she sent to him and to Galaor (see Chapter 57 above), and proves how her prophesies have come true. She concludes her visit by predicting the future, again using a parable, this time involving a lion, a snake, and a fawn, and praising Amadís's role as a very brave knight in the events to come; she thus retains from her earlier appearances the sibylline utterance. All recognize her powers of prophecy and are grateful for her care for them. Having declined to be accompanied, she departs quietly but still enshrouded in mystery: "she went to her ship which having put out to the open sea was engulfed by a great blackness" (II, 519).

Another appearance of Urganda's damsel (this time in Chapter 71) occurs when she again arrives richly dressed on a palfrey but now accompanied by a dwarf on a fine, peach-colored horse—one notes the striking use in these and other episodes of bright colors. They approach Queen Brisena and her ladies on the road and hand over a letter, bearing Urganda's seal and a very beautiful emerald, and tied with golden strings. They then disappear without further ado. This episode recalls earlier examples of Urganda's function as a prophetess and her use of an intermediary. The letter speaks of the young Esplandián, whom Lisuarte has just found and is soon to take with him: he must be well and carefully reared, since he will save the king, he will perform many other good deeds for God, he will be more beloved than any other knight, and he will bring peace between Lisuarte and Amadís.

Urganda now drops out of our story until the conclusion of the events she had prophesied and about which she gave warning. Thus we do not meet her again, apart from two or three passing references to her prophecies, until late in Book IV, some of the last chapters of which she dominates. Here, in Chapter 123, her entrance is again dramatic and unexpected. On the Ínsola Firme, and as the marriages are being arranged, the members of the court are walking in the garden beneath the trees close to the fountains, when they hear great shouting coming from outside. As before, when people are told that something very frightening and strange is coming over the sea, the knights get on their horses and go the shore, while the ladies climb the tower overlooking the sea and the land. First there is seen something even more spectacular than the fires at sea, namely, a very black and frightening cloud of smoke, and then,

a short time after the smoke began to dissipate, they saw in its midst a serpent much bigger than the biggest ship or boat in the world, and it wore such great wings that they took up more space than the distance a bow can shoot, and its tail was curled upward, higher than a great tower. Its head and mouth and teeth were so big and its eyes so frightful that no one would dare to look at it. And from time to time it emitted from its nostrils that very black smoke which went up to heaven and which completely covered everything. It gave such loud and frightful snorts and whistles that the sea itself seemed to sink. It spat out mouthfuls of water so strongly and to such a distance that no ship however big could approach it without foundering. . . . (IV, 1219–20)

This terrifying monster, whose size and appearance have something in common with the Endriago, began to plunge about and stir up the sea and it shook its wings so that the noise of their scales could be heard for a good half league around. As before, the horses took fright but it was thought that a sea creature would not venture onto the land. Then from its side was let down a skiff covered with a very rich golden cloth, and in it was the *dueña* (lady) herself with two very richly dressed youths on whose shoulders she leaned, and there were also two very ugly dwarfs who rowed the skiff to the shore. King Lisuarte knew at once that it was Urganda, since he recalled her earlier visit from the sea—this, we are now told, was at Fenusa, a town in Britain where he held court.

Thus again Urganda makes her appearance by first astonishing and frightening those she is visiting and then ceremoniously and peacefully joining the waiting assembly. On this occasion she appears as herself and not, as the author comments, as she had done earlier, that is, "en figuras estrañas" ("in strange forms"), now as a very old woman, now as a girl. Thus her nickname "la Desconocida" is set aside in these final and fateful appearances, for which that of "Encantadora," or "Enchantress," is more appropriate.

Her first words are for the new emperor of Rome (that is, Arquisil, elected in Chapter 117, after El Patín's defeat and death), and then Amadís, both of whom she praises on their successes and whom she offers to continue to help and advise. They thank her and she then postpones her address to Galaor and Cildadán. After getting the dwarfs to bring three palfreys ashore (meanwhile the court have kept their horses away from the monster!), Urganda proceeds on horseback to the garden, and here she hands over to Esplandián her two youthful attendants (of whom more later).

As before, when Urganda joins the queens and other ladies, who now receive her like no other woman, she exclaims her wonder at their beauty and worth, in particular those of Oriana and Briolanja, of Melicia and Olinda. She is to stay for some days on the Ínsola Firme. In fact, we now pass to Chapter 126 for the sequel to these events, when, after the marriage feasts are over, and the enchantments of the Ínsola are at an end, she speaks to the great assembly about the reason for her visit. Stating that she is only the instrument of God's will—this is not the first or last reference which makes it clear that her (good) magic comes second to a higher dispensation—she addresses Oriana, Amadís, and Lisuarte in turn, in order to show how her prophecies concerning past discords and the discovery of the role of Esplandián in settling them have come true. As for the present ("de que sabiduría no auéys"—"of which you have no knowledge"), she now introduces the fruits of Galaor's and Cildadán's love affairs with her nieces, that is, the youths Talanque and Manelí, to the court, and in particular to Esplandián, as his companions (this we have already discussed). She then says that her Great Serpent (in which, we are reminded, Esplandián is to be armed a knight, that is, in Chapter 133), will be his guide and helper in many future adventures—as is indeed the case in the

Sergas—and he will be known as its knight. These future events are now described again by means of an animal parable involving a falcon and an eagle, and eventually the Serpent will, she declares, sink into the sea, thus showing that from then on Esplandián is to live on dry land.

Finally, on this occasion, and just before her departure, Urganda says she will return for Esplandián's arming and will then prophesy more; further she asks them not to approach the Serpent for fear of being killed, but, it will be recalled, she gives rings to Amadís and Oriana to protect them against Arcaláus, now a prisoner, but kept alive to suffer for his evil deeds. She thanks Amadís for offering again to repay all her favors by saying, significantly, that he has done this already when (as we noted, in Chapter 11 above) Amadís freed her lover, "aquel muy fermoso cauallero, que es la cosa del mundo que yo más amo, aunque él lo haze a mí al contrario" (that is, "that most fair knight who is the thing I most love in the world, although he regards me in the opposite way"). Thus even in her later role as an imposing enchantress and prophetess, the object of every respect and of awe, she retains until the end her other more human role of a woman with a lover. Urganda then boards the Serpent, which is covered in such black smoke for four days that nothing can be seen on it. When this clears, there stands the Serpent, but Urganda has gone.

The last appearance or return of Urganda and her accompanying monster (in Chapter 133) occurs when several of his comrades in arms, for example Balán, Bruneo, Grasandor, and Quadragante, have joined Amadís, on the Ínsola Firme, after hearing that Lisuarte had been taken away by boat across the sea. This would seem to be the work of another enchantress, and it took place after he lost consciousness as he fell in the forest while attending to a damsel in distress. As the knights prepare to go in search of him, Urganda's emergence from the Serpent is announced, although this time she allows herself to be lifted ashore by Galaor. When Oriana bitterly accuses Urganda of not preventing her father's distressing capture, Urganda makes the further significant reply that, since power brings its ups and downs, we must accept the good and the bad if it be God's will. She knew about what has happened to Lisuarte (as in fact she indicated in her parable), but she could not prevent what was ordained; she will however do what she can, with God's help, to remedy this misfortune.

Then, in addressing the assembled knights, she informs them that the liberation of Lisuarte is not to be left to them but to another supplied with special grace from God for the purpose—that is, Esplandián, as is told in Chapter 6 of the *Sergas*. Urganda then invites them all as her guests to the serpent-ship with Esplandián, Talanque, and Manelí, and two other young companions, the King of Dacia and Ambor, son of Angriote. What follows has already been looked at in a little detail above. Suffice it to say here that this ceremony of dedication of Esplandián as a Christian knight is carried out fully in accordance with the hallowed rules of chivalry and the observances of religion. It is not necessary to stress again the importance of these final acts for the ending of the *Amadís* and its continuation in the *Sergas*.

When the morning comes, a very ugly dwarf blows a very loud blast from a trumpet on top of the Serpent and awakens the whole island, bringing out everyone to see what is happening. Urganda then makes all the lords join the dwarf as she follows them but is herself preceded by Esplandián and his four companions. She now asks the reformed giant Balán to make Esplandián a knight, after which, in answer to Urganda's request, Amadís commends to Esplandián his unfulfilled promise to Princess Leonorina (Esplandián's future wife), Queen Menoresa, and others of the court of Constantinople, to send them a knight to serve them. In token of this he gives his son the ring he himself had received from the princess. Esplandián swears by God to do this (as he does in Chapters 49 and following of the *Sergas*), and then he in turn dubs as knights his four young friends. This scene of preparation and dedication, symbolizing the continuation by the younger knights of the work of their elders, ends with the five new knights and all the others falling mysteriously asleep as the six damsels play sweetly on their trumpets. The Great Serpent then disappears into a black and very thick cloud of smoke emitted from its own nostrils.

Shortly afterward the lords find themselves in the garden where Urganda had first met them, and when the smoke clears the Serpent is not to be seen nor is there any sign of Esplandián and the other young knights (they of course reappear at the beginning of the *Sergas*). It seems to all that it is a dream, but then Amadís finds a letter in his hand. In this, sent it would appear by Urganda, the kings and lords are requested to rest and give up combat, and Amadís in particular is asked to prepare himself for the new and dangerous responsibilities of a ruler, for his son will take over his triumphs in arms as foreordained, and he will even eclipse Amadís in fame and glory. Amadís advises them all to let their experience of Urganda and her powers give them hope that, if God wills, she will find a remedy for what is to come. They should therefore depart each to his own land, and Queen Brisena should be told the reason for their decision, while she in her turn will let them know her wishes in due course. They all agree to do this and to stand ready to help whenever news of Lisuarte is known.

This long and varied episode dominated by Urganda ends the book and leaves the reader with the clear impression that an unfinished story has in a way been rounded off but that it will be taken up later, since all has somehow been left in the hands of superior forces. We thus leave the *Amadís* at the level of beneficent control and of hope in God, not of pure chance.

Urganda, then, is no mere enchantress but a prophetess, intercessor, and guide, while also possessing a rather protean nature, as a girl or an old woman. Later her role as a great interpreter with her explanations and her sibylline forecasts turns her into the intermediary presiding, in a highly moral fashion, over the present and the future actions of the main characters of the *Amadís*. It can be suggested at this point that Urganda's career is derived from more than two Breton sources (and she does recall several older figures), since her role as a woman of different forms or ages, including a woman in love, is radically distinct from her later one as *dea ex machina* of the fateful events that conclude the *Amadís*. Montalvo may thus here, as elsewhere, have evolved an original version of older material. Urganda helps but also leaves men and women to follow their nature and conscience, and she declares herself repeatedly as under God and subject to His will and providence, while she also warns about such evil forces as Arcaláus. Urganda praises Amadís unreservedly on several occasions while also regarding Esplandián almost as the hope of the world; indeed, through her grandnephews she identifies herself closely with his future.

At no point does Urganda use her magical powers basely or needlessly. Her majestic final scenes, as a *dueña* (or kind of sea goddess) in possession of awe-inspiring accompaniments and of truly regal presence, underline the serious religious emphasis which has been seen as typical of the latter part of the novel. Her wisdom, that is, her proven powers of prophecy, is widely and continuously recognized and praised by those whom she counsels and aids. Her role in the *Amadís* grows noticeably and eventually becomes a dominant one, as, it seems, that of a being who mediates between weak man and the otherwise inscrutable providence of God. Urganda is therefore an integral part of the meaning of the last version of our romance. This, it is to be hoped, justifies a rather extended treatment of her role in this analysis of different aspects of the contents of the *Amadís*. Urganda, of course, also plays a prominent role in the *Sergas*, in which there occurs, for example, the interesting authorial device (in Chapters 98 and 99) of Montalvo, in two visions, being told by her to give up and then to resume his telling of the story.

II   *Arcaláus*

Arcaláus is by comparison a puny, almost contemptible figure, and we have already seen how the author makes him the subject of others' fun, as if to reduce his impact. Indeed, as already stated, he soon ceases to be an enchanter and becomes much more the wily but ineffectual intriguer and opponent in arms of Lisuarte and Amadís, until he is finally rewarded by the humiliation of a caged confinement. Since his later activities have been referred to in some detail already, a selective account of his overall role is all that is called for here. Arcaláus's early career and name make him reminiscent of certain minor characters in the Breton cycle, such as Arc-à-l'eau or Archelaus—as Miss Williams has pointed out—although he emerges in the *Amadís* as a clearly original creation. (Archelaus is by the way also the name of two early Christian saints!)

This enchanter's decision to oppose Amadís by making him a victim of crude physical impediment is that of an old-style villain or common wizard. Thus, having heard of Arcaláus and of his evil deeds for the first time from Ardián the dwarf, whose master the enchanter had killed, Amadís gets involved (in the same Chapter 18) with Arcaláus in his own castle. Here Amadís frees Grindalaya, also beloved of King Arbán de Norgales (of North Wales), his friend, and kills the jailor; here also Arcaláus had carried off the lady in a black cloud and cast her in chains into a dungeon. Amadís then fights Arcaláus, who in fear of his life, and when he gets his attacker into a room, also enchants him so that he falls into a deep sleep. He then puts on Amadís's armor, makes out that the latter is dead, locks up

Gandalín, the dwarf, and the others, and rides off on Amadís's horse to Lisuarte's court. His plans are, however, brought to nothing, since (in Chapter 19) his wife, a good and virtuous woman, who always prays for his reformation, has Amadís disenchanted. This is done with the help of two damsels and a magic book which when divided into four parts is burned and Amadís is then asked to rise from his trance (it will be recalled that Urganda also made use of a book, but to put people to sleep). Amadís then frees all of Arcaláus's victims and himself goes off in pursuit. Arcaláus, however, as we know, gets to Lisuarte first (in Chapter 20) and spreads the false reports of Amadís's death, and then departs. Soon, however, Grindalaya in turn arrives and tells them the whole, true story.

As we have also seen above, Arcaláus had a willing helper in his beautiful niece Dinarda. Another such relative (an unnamed niece), however, suffers decapitation by one of Arcaláus's former prisoners, Baláys de Carsante, when, as we recall (in Chapter 22), she tells him that she had instigated the mortal combat between Amadís and Galaor—who do not recognize each other—and which Baláys now stops just in time. Thus had Arcaláus managed to sow discord among the protagonists early in Book I, as a result of which he became an object of hatred and of malediction. Soon after this he persuades King Barsinán, in the first of his attempts to work with allies and dupes, to usurp the kingdom of Great Britain. There then follow the events of which we already know (from Chapter 31 to Chapter 38): first the treachery of Barsinán, then the equally treacherous capture of Lisuarte and Oriana and their imprisonment, followed by Oriana's freeing by Amadís after his fierce combat with Arcaláus, then Lisuarte's liberation by Galaor, Barsinán's actual treason, savagery, defeat, and death, and also that of his companion, Arcaláus's cousin, by burning alive. Thus Arcaláus's villainous attempt to overthrow Lisuarte and his kingdom, both regarded at that point as the epitome of the chivalrous virtues, fails because of the great bravery of Amadís, Galaor, and others, although his malevolence is increased by his use and sacrifice of the ambitious Barsinán and his own cousin, while Arcaláus himself escapes, at least for the moment. Most of this multiple act of treachery moves on the natural plane of combat and rescue, but, at the time of the arrival of Barsinán in Lisuarte's court (in Chapter 32), Arcaláus performs an ignoble piece of magic by stealing the crown and mantle from Queen Brisena's little chest, as noted above.

Arcaláus thus appears increasingly in the role of an evil schemer and murderous conspirator, who again uses others for his evil designs. Later (in Chapter 50) Guilán has to defend himself and Amadís's shield, which he is guarding, from attacks by Arcaláus's two nephews, one of whom he kills while the other flees. Shortly afterward (in Chapter 54) he is listed by the strange knight in his challenge to Lisuarte and his court as among the latter's greatest enemies. Soon after this Amadís misses another chance to settle with Arcaláus, when (in Chapter 57) he kills in combat, for assaulting Oriana, his nephew Lindoraque, but fails to catch up with the fleeing and defeated Arcaláus. We meet him, or rather a reference to him, only later when (in Chapter 67) he is described as the plotter (the Spanish word used, "urdir," to warp or scheme, is very apt) in stirring up the lords of the islands under the leadership of his new ally Arábigo, king of the Islands of Landas and of Arabia, against Lisuarte in the latter's struggle with Galvanes and Madasima. (It will be noted that Arcaláus's new ally and one of his kingdoms bear names from the traditional enemies of medieval Christendom, and it will be recalled that in Carolingian romance the struggle with Islam was a central theme.) This fresh campaign of Arcaláus does indeed come to a great battle (in Chapter 68), which is a dress rehearsal for his final and most fateful act of treachery and which, as we know, almost succeeds.

Soon after (in Chapter 69), when Perión and his sons are returning to Gaul after helping Lisuarte in this battle, they are induced by a very beautiful damsel, playing dumb, and who is none other than Dinarda, to accompany her to Arcaláus's palace. Here next morning they find their lavishly appointed bedchamber buried, by means of what looks like an ingenious piece of technological magic, in the bowels of the castle. Thus trapped and threatened with death by Arcaláus, Dinarda gets them some food and drink and eventually they are saved by Gandalín and others who work the mechanism to bring them up to the surface again. Then all of them release the other prisoners and fight and defeat Arcaláus and his men, setting fire to the castle. Arcaláus later meets Galaor and Norandel, but is again defeated and escapes only by claiming a false identity as Granfil. There then follows the amorous adventure already known to us and involving these last two knights and Dinarda and her damsel. This adventure, recalling earlier kidnapping and treacherous capture by Arcaláus, ends for the moment his active role in the *Amadís*.

In Book IV, as we know, Arcaláus makes his last and almost

successful attempt. A summary will again suffice. We meet him (in Chapter 96) when, "esperando siempre de hazer algún mal" ("hoping always to do some evil"), he first hears of the discord between Lisuarte and Amadís and is, of course, overjoyed, since these are the two men he most dislikes and whom he never ceases to wish to destroy. The enmity of Lisuarte and Amadís seems to give him an opportunity to finish off them and their armies at the same time. Again, as we know, he approaches the willing Arábigo, to whom this time are added Barsinán's son of the same name ("mancebo muy orgulloso"—"a very haughty youth"), the family of Dardán—whom Amadís had killed previously—and the king of the Profunda Ínsola (Deep Island). Thus all of Lisuarte's and Amadís's old enemies are to make common cause in this last endeavor to overcome the established forces of law and order, for the moment unhappily divided. Later (in Chapter 98) we are given the full details of the drawing up and assembling of the hosts of Arcaláus and his allies from a vantage point on a mountain. Much later again (in Chapter 115), that is, after the great decisive battle and the defeat and death of El Patín and Lisuarte's humiliation, followed by the intercession of Esplandián and Nasciano and the truce between Amadís and Lisuarte, the last named is on his way with his defeated and exhausted forces to his town of Lubaina in Great Britain, when Arcaláus and his allies decide to first defeat one and then the other of their enemies. Lisuarte has wind of the ambush on the mountain and calls on all his own allies to be ready to stand and fight, although he refuses to alert Perión, Amadís, and their host, since, as the author comments, he looks to his honor rather than to his own safety.

Arcaláus and his company attack as Lisuarte is close to Lubaina (in Chapter 116), and the latter's fate seems sealed. However, we know how by chance Esplandián arrives and sees what is about to happen and then returns with Perión, Amadís, and their army, but not before Lisuarte and his men are almost defeated, as the fighting extends to the streets of the city. Then at the last moment, when all seems lost, Amadís and his companions arrive (in Chapter 117), surround Lubaina, and attack Arcaláus and his force from behind. We also know the rest: the enemy is heavily defeated, Arcaláus and Arábigo are spared but imprisoned, and Arcaláus promises restitution for all his wrongdoing, to which Amadís replies that he hopes his captivity will chasten and reform him.

Amid the rejoicing and reconciliation that follow we do not hear of Arcaláus again until Chapter 130, when Amadís, during the subsequent adventures on the Ínsola de la Torre Bermeja (Island of the Red Tower), comes across Arcaláus's wife, whom we met as a good woman in Chapter 19, when she had Amadís disenchanted and freed. (The reader will also recall that the wife of the giant Bandaguido, evil father of the Endriago—in Chapter 73—was herself a good woman who tried to undo her husband's wickedness; she, however, also became his victim). Arcaláus's wife, on her knees before Amadís, begs him to grant her a request; and this, it turns out, is to hand Arcaláus to her so that she can take him to safety. Amadís reluctantly agrees to help this sorrowful wife even at the risk of letting Arcaláus loose again, such is the former's sense of duty as a knight. They find Arcaláus in a sorry state although still fierce (and we also recall that he had been given a good book to read!) and determined to see his punishment through. No request for restitution or reform or respect for God's law by Amadís is now listened to, since Arcaláus rightly says that Amadís is not freeing him willingly. This evil man remains unrepentant to the end and even shows ingratitude toward his wife whom, however, the author praises as a prototype of the good mother and spouse who can hold a family together. Cursing Urganda la Desconocida (as a "mala puta," or "evil whore"), Arcaláus goes on his way with his family, warning Amadís to be careful since he will soon seek revenge for his unjust imprisonment.

Thus, like other such characters in older romances, or indeed like his successor, Conan Doyle's Professor Moriarty, in a much more recent romance, Arcaláus lives to fight and to do evil another day. He owes his freedom not to the magic he used upon his enemies but to a saintly woman's persistent love and to a knight's high sense of honor. In this way his innate and, it seems, irredeemable malevolence is, at the end of our story as often before, set against the virtues which sustain the *Amadís*. Arcaláus has something of the dimensions of a rounded character, and he shows a perverse dignity and pride which fit his insolence in a manner typical of the devil himself as so often portrayed in literature. That is, Arcaláus is portrayed mostly as a moral monster, and this fact makes him more credible than if he had been presented simply as a wizard.

III   *The Ínsola Firme*

The third main area of magic in the *Amadís* concerns, of course, the Ínsola Firme, that region which, as again Miss Williams has shown, recalls such similar places from the Breton cycle as the Val

sans Retour (Valley without Return) or Val des faux Amants (Valley
of False Lovers), the Joyeuse Garde (Joyous Guard), and the
Douloureuse Garde (the Dolorous Guard). The several symbolical
meanings suggested by this island and its position will be considered
later. Suffice it to say here that as a place of magical properties its
enchantments stand apart from the varieties practiced by Urganda
and Arcaláus. The magical events on this island belong to the first
unnumbered chapter and other parts of Book II, although it is, as we
know, to play a large part in Books III and IV as the haven and later
the seat and abode of Amadís and others. It will also be remembered
that Apolidón (a prince of great wisdom and wizardry) and his beloved Grimanesa had made of the island an abode of great delights
and joys and that they left it only when they were called back to
Greece to become its emperor and empress. They leave their happy
home of sixteen years by ensuring that it will in future be ruled over
only by someone who is their equal "así en fortaleza de armas como
en lealtad de amores y de sobrada fermosura" ("both in strength of
arms and loyalty of love and of surpassing beauty"). This is done by
the invention of physical tests that draw on moral qualities as much
as a show of bravery, and they are described as of almost bewilder-
ing detail (a rather longer account than that given in our Chapter 2
above is called for here).

Thus at the entrance to an orchard with all kinds of trees there
was placed an arch and in the garden were built four rooms or
chambers of great richness. The orchard was so surrounded that it
could be entered only through the arch on which was the copper
effigy of a man with a trumpet to his mouth. Within the orchard
there was also a palace which contained two figures in the living
likeness of Apolidón and Grimanesa, and with a very bright jasper
stone at their side. There was also erected about half a crossbow's
shot from the arch and in a large open field an iron column five
forearms in length. Apolidón then declared that only pure lovers
could go through the arch, otherwise those trying to enter would be
paralyzed and then expelled by the effigy blowing an awful blast on
his trumpet and with smoke of fire, and then left as dead. The pure
or loyal lovers would be received with a very sweet sound and they
would see the figures of Apolidón and Grimanesa and find their
names written by they know not whom on the jasper stone. Apolidón and Grimanesa then successfully tried out their inventions, but
several of their ladies and damsels and knights fared ill, all to

Grimanesa's amusement. As for the rich room where she and Apolidón had had such pleasure, Apolidón had two columns, one of stone and the other of copper, placed at five paces from the door and five further on respectively. Only he who surpasses him in arms and she who surpasses her in beauty can safely enter here. On the copper column Apolidón had an inscription made allowing knights of great valor to pass, and on the stone one an inscription allowing him to pass who surpasses Apolidón, and this last man will then be lord of the island.

Furthermore, his magic is so arranged that no one can approach the room closer than twelve paces or enter it except by way of the two columns. He further ordered that the Ínsola Firme be ruled by a governor who would also collect its revenues—used later, it will be recalled, by Amadís to found a monastery—and keep them for the knight who might enter the room and become its new master. This knight was to be served only by those who passed the test of the Lovers' Arch, and Apolidón also ordered that those who could not pass the copper column should leave their arms there, and that those who succeeded should take only their swords, while those who got to the marble column should take only their shields, but that if they could still not enter the room they should take their spurs. Ladies and damsels were to take nothing with them but simply to say their names and place them on the door of the castle, indicating how far each had gone. Finally, Apolidón declared that all this enchantment would disappear for those knights who freely passed through the columns and entered the room, but that this would happen for the women only when she came who would end it with her great beauty and dwell in the room with the knight who would have won the lordship of the island.

Unlike the early simple mystification and the later rather terrifying and spectacular magic of Urganda, or the ignoble use of a trance and a disappearing trick by Arcaláus to confound his victims, the enchantments of the Ínsola Firme operate amid most pleasant, indeed luxurious surroundings, and are clearly meant to symbolize the virtues of chivalry and the purity of true love. These enchantments act to set apart the special natures and the exceptional dedication of our hero and heroine. It is surely significant that the Ínsola Firme and its mysteries are presented early in our romance when Amadís and Oriana have already shown their qualities in Book I and just before the first of their major trials, that is, as a result of

Oriana's jealousy. It will be recalled that the author also points out that the importance of the Ínsola Firme in Book IV justifies his inclusion of an account of it at this stage in Book II.

In the second (and numbered) chapter of Book II, that is, Chapter 44, and in an episode whose details typify much of the *Amadís*, Amadís and his brothers together with his cousin Agrajes, having reinstated Queen Briolanja, are on their way to Lisuarte's court. As they pause to pray in a hermitage, a damsel offers to take them to the Ínsola Firme close by the open sea and to see its marvels, of which they have already heard. They are then to try their fortunes as loyal lovers. Accompanied by its governor, Isanjo, they reach the island, now described as being seven leagues long and five wide (later, in Chapter 63, it is said to be nine leagues by seven), and as deriving its name from its proximity to the mainland. On arrival they see signs, in the shape of many shields, left at the point where their bearers could penetrate no further, of those who had tried the tests, and among these shields Amadís recognizes the emblems of Arcaláus, Abiés of Ireland, whom Amadís had killed, and Quadragante, Abiés's brother and later Amadís's friend.

Agrajes tries first and gets as far as the effigies of Apolidón and Grimanesa; he is followed by Amadís—the others objecting that they are not dedicated lovers—and this makes the trumpeter on the arch react more favorably. Agrajes at this point fails to get Amadís to reveal his love, and he and Amadís begin to look at the delights of the place. The brothers Florestán and Galaor try to join them but each in turn is met with so many and such unbearable blows with swords and lances that he gets no further than the columns and is then cast out of the orchard more dead than alive. Amadís, who now sees his name written on the jasper stone, returns with Agrajes to succor his brothers. Agrajes's attempt to avenge the latter is met with the same fate as they suffered, but Amadís, commending himself to Oriana, for whom he does it, also finds that his attack on the enchantments is met with great resistance, even if he just manages to reach the magic chamber. Here he is taken in by a mysterious big, hard hand and told he is welcome as the new lord of the island, at which he recovers his strength and thanks Oriana for his success. His lordship is now recognized by all and his brothers are also shown the wonders of the chamber and especially the room of Apolidón and Grimanesa, which is built in such a way that those inside can see what goes on outside but not vice versa. Amadís, now proclaimed as the first new ruler in the hundred years since Apolidón's departure, and his brothers join with the rest in rejoicing and feasting. At this point the author reflects on how even for Amadís his present glory and happiness will change to ill fortune and grief, which will eventually, however, with God's will, be changed to a new happiness. This proves to be most apposite, for, as we have said, the victory by Amadís the perfect lover is immediately followed by Oriana's angry and jealous letter which is to bring him close to despair.

Oriana, however, does not enter the Ínsola Firme until much later, but a little after the above events (in Chapter 56), when Amadís still goes under his name of Beltenebrós and Oriana herself is disguised with a mask, they both successfully pass magical tests at Lisuarte's court. These, as we know, consist first of the wonderfully wrought sword, part of it very hard and bright and part very red and burning, in the green scabbard, itself magnificently adorned, and second of the headdress of very beautiful flowers, one half of them as fresh and green as if newly cut as they blossom, and the other half so dry that they might crumble at the touch. These are brought to court by the aged squire Macandón, nephew of Apolidón, who had made a promise to his mother that he would allow himself to become a knight only at the hands of the world's most loyal lover and would take his sword from the hands of the truest damsel or lady. His uncle, being unable to dub him since Grimanesa was then dead, gave him the headdress and the sword, of which the scabbard had come from the bone of serpents living in a hot and green sea between India and Tartary, while the headdress was from trees on an island in the sea of Tartary also very remote and dangerous. Macandón says that he who unsheathes the sword will turn both halves of it bright and clear, and that she who loves her knight so well will on placing them on her head make the dry flowers as beautiful as the others.

These two tests are, as we know, won by our hero and heroine (in Chapter 57), that is, after Amadís's brothers and others fail to draw out the sword—over which Amadís now makes the sign of the cross—and equally after others, including Queens Brisena and Briolanja, fail to restore the dry flowers to their original beauty. Then Amadís makes Macandón a knight at long last, and Briolanja compliments Oriana on the strength of the love which she and her lover share. Amadís and Oriana, still unrecognized, then leave. This

mid-story triumph of the hero and heroine prefigures their final
union and joy and stands as an achievement which will sustain them
both in the new separation and distress that are to follow. For the
moment at least Oriana joins Amadís as the other most loyal lover
and is declared the most beautiful lady.

The Ínsola Firme is later (in Chapter 63) visited by Queen
Briolanja and her ladies when they witness more of its wonders and
attractions. This episode, however, is related in the third person to
Oriana by Briolanja's damsel (it will be recalled that this was seen, in
our Chapter 4, as a good example of the structural device of bringing
together two narrative strands), and thus provides Oriana with a
second indirect acquaintance with her future abode. These fresh
marvels are shown to Briolanja and her retinue from the vantage
point of a fine tower in what had been one of Apolidón's palaces.
From a dark, deep cave there emerges a frightful serpent spouting
smoke and lashing its tail; then come out two lions which begin a
savage fight, scattering all those standing nearby. When the lions lie
exhausted, the serpent carries them one by one into the cave.

Later that night, when the ladies are asleep in their lavish
chambers, they are rudely awakened as a black and white stag enters with lighted candles on its horns, and followed by four dogs
looking like it and worrying it, and after them an ivory horn being
blown as if for the hunt and moving as if it were in someone's hand.
The harried stag flees to the other end of the chamber, jumping over
the beds and falling over them, at which the ladies also flee and
hide, until finally the stag leaves by a window, followed by the dogs.

Next day they visit a round marble house on twelve marble posts
in the forest: once within its finely wrought doors, locked with glass
keys, one can see what goes on outside, but inside stand copper
effigies of giants which with their bows and arrows of fire burn to
ashes anyone or anything that enters. Briolanja and her ladies then
see two bucks and a crow put inside and killed with arrows of fire.
On the door an inscription forbids any man or woman to enter,
unless they love as loyally as Apolidón and Grimanesa, who set up
this enchantment, and they must also enter together. This enchantment and all the others will last until such a knight and such a
lady enter the room and make love, when all such magic in the
Ínsola Firme will be undone. Insanjo in explanation can only say
that the first two magical events happen each day and that the stag
and the dogs end up in a lake.

Finally, the next day, Briolanja, who has until now delayed doing so, rides to the Lovers' Arch and alone of her company negotiates it and reaches the effigies and finds her name on the jasper stone. On the fifth day, richly dressed, she attacks the forbidden chamber, but, having passed the columns, she is there dragged back by the hair. Briolanja's experiences on the Ínsola Firme contain two episodes of magic that are strictly nonfunctional and simply adorn the narrative, and in fact strangely recall Urganda's animal parables of violence. The third episode, however, adds to what we know of the Ínsola Firme and shows that Briolanja is not quite the lady being awaited to end the magic and its tests.

Immediately afterward (still in Chapter 63) we are told how Amadís and his companions arrive again at the Ínsola Firme and are happily received by its inhabitants. When they see its strong castle and how the island has but one approach, and also how rich and well populated it is, they conclude that it could challenge all the world to war. This or something like it is to be the island's role later in the *Amadís*. The hero and his knights then visit the same dwellings Briolanja saw and also the spinning house and the bull's house, from the latter of which a raging bull is brought out, tamed by an old monkey riding on its back. We are then told that these and other enchantments, which pleased all the knights, had been invented by Apolidón for Grimanesa's entertainment. Thus the magical events, witnessed also by Briolanja, are seen to use animals and even architecture for very special spectacles, perhaps not totally unlike those enjoyed by medieval royalty. Animals are also met with in the older romances and associated with magic.

A passing but not insignificant reference to the Ínsola Firme occurs much later (in Chapter 74), when Princess Leonorina gives Amadís her lovely ring, half burning ruby, half white ruby, much more precious than one of red ruby or of emerald. The emperor tells Amadís how Apolidón was his grandfather and Amadís then reminds him of how the Ínsola Firme was won by Amadís and of its present state (Amadís, it will be recalled, lives incognito at the Greek court). The emperor then tells how Leonorina's stone has its mate in one of her crowns and that they originally formed one stone, which had been given to Grimanesa by Apolidón, but that she had insisted that one half be separated and given for love to her husband. The emperor comments that another will get it from Amadís and indeed this, as we know, will be Esplandián, who carries out his father's pledge, returns the ring to Leonorina, and eventually marries her. Thus the Ínsola Firme has woven another bond of unity and love around Amadís and his family.

The enchantment of the Ínsola Firme, which, as we can see, plays a role comparable to that of Urganda, is encountered once more toward the end of the *Amadís*, when in fact Amadís and Oriana eventually enter upon their inheritance as the two perfect lovers. This takes place fittingly (in Chapter 125) just after all the marriages have been solemnized by Nasciano, and when Amadís asks Lisuarte to get Oriana to agree to pass the tests, beginning with the Lovers' Arch and as far as the prohibited chamber, which latter only Amadís has entered, as we recall. Oriana agrees, but she is impetuously preceded by two other new brides, namely, Melicia and Olinda. These latter indeed pass safely underneath and reach the room with the effigies. Then follows the modest and rather frightened Oriana, who causes a flood of flowers to pour from the trumpet and the sweetest of sounds to be emitted, and then she joins the other two to admire the effigies, especially that of the most beautiful Grimanesa. The three are now joined by their husbands, Amadís, Agrajes, and Bruneo, who had already passed the initial tests. When they decide to try the test of the special chamber, the beautiful Grasinda (now Quadragante's wife) goes in first, but when she gets as far as the marble column she is rudely and violently expelled. The same happens to Melicia and Olinda, but Oriana, when led in by Amadís, finally arrives at the chamber exhausted, like Amadís; she is brought in by the mysterious hand, and is told by a chorus of more than twenty voices that she has surpassed Grimanesa, and that she and Amadís will rule the island for many years.

Then the governor Isanjo declares that the entire enchantment of the orchard has been dissolved, as Apolidón the inventor wished, with the arrival of his two successors. The result is that Amadís and Oriana now invite everyone freely to visit the chamber and its wonders, and then arrange for the marriage feast to be held within. Thus this special magic, which sought out a kind of human perfection, has served its purpose and the great competition is over. Love has been well served by enchantment which has exalted it, just as Urganda's astonishing appearances have underpinned the aspirations and confirmed the achievements of both knights and lovers.

IV   *The Letters*

A subsidiary form of magic concerns the mysterious letters discovered by the Damsel of Denmark and Mabilia on Esplandián's breast at his birth (in Chapter 66). Underneath the right nipple there were letters as white as snow, while under the left one were seven others as red as live coals (one should again note the use of bright and contrasting colors in situations related to magic and mystery). The letters were indiscipherable to the two women, since the white were in very obscure Latin and the red in "muy cerrado" ("very hermetic") Greek. When, however, the child is rescued from the lioness and taken to Naciano, the latter, seeing the letters, reads the Latin ones as "Esplandián" and baptizes the boy with this name. As for the red letters, Nasciano has no more luck than the damsels in reading them.

The unnatural phenomenon of the letters on his breast as well as his taking by the lioness recall, as Miss Williams has shown, earlier cases in the Breton cycle, the *Gran Conquista*, and even ancient classical legend. More specifically, Lancelot's cousin Lionel had a birthmark in the form of a lion—hence the name he was given. Esplandián's letters, which so obviously symbolize the importance of their possessor's origin and his later role in Greece and in its defense, also give the author an early opportunity to forecast his great future, and again become an important topic toward the end of the *Amadís*. This occurs (in Chapter 133, during the very last adventures of Amadís) when the latter is still on the Ínsola de la Torre Bermeja, of his enemy the giant Balán, and with Grasandor, and when they meet Nalfón, Queen Madasima's majordomo. This last then tells them the story of the Peña de la Doncella Encantadora (the Rock of the Damsel Enchantress), which, with its sequel, as will be seen, has details recalling other incidents in our romance.

This rock in the sea once belonged to an enchantress who lived on it in great splendor and also used it to harass and capture ships' crews as they passed by, until one day she fell in love with one of her captives, a Cretan, whom, however, she would not let go. He then threw her into the sea and escaped, leaving her great treasure locked up in a room of her palace. This last is now the abode of serpents and can only be opened by the knight who is named on the door in two sets of letters, one white, the other blood red, and who will pull out a sword buried up to the hilt in the doors.

A little later Amadís and Grasandor are led over the sea to the rock where, after much toil and climbing, they reach a hermitage, inside of which is a statue which presses against its breast a large tablet containing large letters in Greek (the enchantress herself had come from Argos) legible even after two hundred years. After resting from the climb, Amadís is able to read the letters, since he had learned the language while in Greece and also from Elisabad on his return journey. The inscription runs thus: when the great island, presumably the Ínsola Firme, or Great Britain, is eventually ruled by a powerful king and becomes mistress of all, there will be joined together great and unparalleled achievement in arms and the flower of beauty, and from this union will emerge he who will draw forth the sword to complete his commitment to chivalry, and then too the strong stone doors enclosing the great treasure will be opened. Wondering and doubting about the import of all this, Amadís and Grasandor climb up higher to see if they can complete the adventure. Again after much effort they reach the ruined buildings of the former palaces and go under a stone arch on top of which is a perfectly made stone effigy of a damsel. The latter has a stone pen in her right hand and in her left a sign with Greek letters saying that true wisdom is that which profits us with the gods rather than with men, and the rest is vanity.

Amadís and Grasandor enter a great yard with fountains and more ruined buildings and caves with snakes in them. Well armed and at the ready, they enter the houses and a great domed room, and at the end of this are more stone doors tight shut and with a sword driven to the hilt into their intersection. Thus they arrive at the treasure chamber, where the work on the sword and its colors amaze them. On the right of one door are seven well-chiseled blood-red letters, and on the left seven whiter than the stone, in Latin. These last say: in vain will any knight try to draw forth the sword unless it be he who points to the letters written on the sign and joins with them the seven letters red as a fire which he has on his breast. This adventure is being kept for him by the damsel who knew that his equal would not come in his day or afterward. (We recall here that, in Chapter 126, Urganda also told Esplandián that after many afflictions his letters would be read.) Amadís thus realizes that it is reserved for his son, although he and Grasandor cannot read the blood-red letters. After assuring themselves that there is no other way into the chamber, they leave the rock and its mystery to Esplandián.

Thus a significant episode, involving enchantment of a kind somewhat reminiscent of the Ínsola Firme, ends with the one clear withdrawal of Amadís from an adventure in the entire *Amadís*. In fact, the adventure is completed in the first two chapters of the *Sergas* when Esplandián wins the sword and enters the wonderful chamber where again an inscription foretells his future glory and tasks. In this way enchantment takes up the apparently loose thread of Esplandián's lettering and leads it into the sequel of Montalvo. In this it also complements the role played by Urganda at the end of the *Amadís* and during the *Sergas*.

Some considerable space has been given to the role of magic in our romance because of its clear relevance to the actual narrative flow as well as to the underlying meaning of the story. Like some aspects of the subject of love, it has pre-Christian origins, but both have clearly been developed within Montalvo's moralistic interpretation of the story. The nature and the disposal of the material involving enchantment can also be said to illustrate the practice of interweaving. Thus the interrelationships of Amadís, Urganda, Galaor, and Esplandián, and the reappearance and disappearance of the topic of Esplandián's birth letters and of the knowledge possessed by Urganda of this phenomenon. Fantasy, the supernatural, physical prowess, and moral endeavor all combine to give life to enchantment, which in any case formed a topic of much discussion for contemporary writers and which also was believed to be a power possessed by devils and even by magicians.[1]

V   *Symbolism and Dreams*

A shorter account will be given of the associated matters of symbolism and dreams. The former has been referred to on more than one occasion and obviously forms part of all the main activities and topics represented in the novel. For example, the recurrence of magic and mystery at once causes symbolism to emerge because of the very relationship of the natural and the unnatural spheres of existence in the same story. It is therefore necessary to limit our coverage of symbolism mainly to the use of certain objects or situations in which it is employed to deepen the meaning of the narrative—again with plenty of precedents in older romance.

For example, arms, and in particular the sword (the traditional symbol of a knight's valor and honor), come up in the story from time to time in a special way. Thus very early on (in Chapter I) King

Perión, placing his right hand on the hilt, or crosslike part, of his sword, swears by the order of chivalry to do Elisena's commands and in particular to become her husband; this is later recalled, in the same chapter, by Elisena, but only as a private, not a public, oath, and thus she is also to keep secret her pregnancy and Amadís's birth. Again, Amadís, early in his adventures as a new knight (in Chapter 21), receives from the young Princess Briolanja her father's richly worked sword when he offers to avenge her against Abíseos, and he is asked to use it for her love. Later (in Chapter 38), Amadís makes good use of Lisuarte's sword to defeat the usurping Barsinán, and to show his regard for this weapon he addresses it after the victory as the best in the world, particularly since he is then also wearing a rusty helmet and carrying a faded shield.

Shortly afterward (in Chapter 40), Amadís at last finds himself in a position to carry out his vow to Briolanja to avenge her father's death, but the sword she had given him has been broken into three pieces in a combat with Gasinán (in Chapter 27); these pieces he told Gandalín to keep and to bring with him, but Ardián the dwarf has left them behind and Amadís now sends him to fetch them. This act, by which he clearly intends to show his acknowledgment of her gift and to remind himself of his vow, also, as we know, causes the dwarf to think that Amadís loves Briolanja and to say so to Oriana, which in turn gives rise to her jealousy.

Later again, Guilán, after having failed to find the distracted Amadís, brings his arms to court (in Chapter 50), where he displays in particular his shield, thus causing both astonishment and grief in all. In this way we have the double symbolism, that of the abandonment of the weapons by the knight as he becomes a hermit, and that of their recovery as outward signs of Amadís's personality. It would perhaps be stretching our relatively simple meaning of symbolism to stress the account of Macandón's green sword won by Amadís as Beltenebrós, or the accompanying flowered headdress won by Oriana (in Chapter 56), but at least they do stand for his and her steadfastness and true love. Equally (in Chapter 68) the presenting by Urganda of the shields to Perión and his two sons has a certain symbolical value in underlining their worth and bravery.

The ring is another object of clear symbolical meaning in the *Amadís*. We have already mentioned how (in Chapter 1) Perión leaves Elisena a ring as a token of his love. This same ring, as well as Perión's sword, is deposited with the short letter bearing the child

Amadís's name in the ark thrown into the sea (in the same chapter), and these two objects are to act as signs of his origin, as Gandales, his rescuer, quickly realizes. Later (in Chapter 14), Oriana, in arranging a tryst with Amadís, sends to him with Gandalín her favorite ring, which her lover kisses and presses to his heart. In Chapter 35, as Amadís and Oriana and their company seek the shade from the heat of the day, on their way back from the bloody affray in which Amadís has liberated her from Arcaláus, he proposes that they send for food to the neighboring town and that they give the horse in exchange for it; Oriana, however, in a simple and aristocratic act of generosity, offers her ring to Gandalín as payment for the badly needed sustenance. While he is away, we recall, the lovers consummate their passion.

We also recall the lively and charming episode (in Chapter 74) when Princess Leonorina of Constantinople gives Amadís her ring which contains half of the very beautiful stone (the other half being in her crown) originally divided by Grimanesa and Apolidón. This is to be a token of the service Amadís promised to this lovely young woman, and this promise he passes on to Esplandián (in Chapter 133) together with Leonorina's ring; Esplandián indeed redeems his father's undertaking when as his successor, in the *Sergas*, he visits the Greek court and eventually marries the princess. We also have seen, late too in the book (in Chapter 126), the solemn and symbolic presentation by Urganda to Amadís and Oriana of two rings which will protect them against the wiles of Arcaláus.

The magic ring is, of course, a very common topic in romance and folklore. The uses to which the ring is put in our novel are certainly to be found in much other literature, but the simple symbolism involved makes its own addition to the interest and meaning of the story. Apart from these two objects of common wear and clearly symbolical value in many tales, there are no others which appear with any regularity. There is, however, the single but striking little detail (in Chapter 30) of Lisuarte seating Amadís, Galaor, Galvanes, and Agrajes alone at the one dinner table, to illustrate—as the author makes explicit—the many dangers and setbacks to be undergone together by these four inseparable companions. Very brief mention might also be made of the use of gloves by Oriana (in Chapter 33) to indicate to Amadís, when they are with the queen and her ladies, that he has Oriana's permission to leave with a damsel who has recently come to ask for his help. This is again a simple but quite effective example of the symbolical act, used here and at a time when the two lovers have not made their love public.

As stated above, much symbolizing can be detected throughout the *Amadís,* given its subject matter and treatment. To try to cover the topic in all its manifestations would lead to repetition of much material already examined under other headings, such as names, love, magic, and religion.[2]

Dreams deserve a few special words. They, even more than magic or enchantment, have played a significant role in literature of all ages, indeed since their use in Genesis for the story of Joseph and the Pharaoh. As employed in the *Amadís* they will be familiar to any reader of epic or romance. Thus, they come to people as premonitions or revelations of one kind or another, sometimes requiring special interpretation, and, of course, they also provide a distinctive dramatic flavor to the narrative.

Very early in the novel (in Chapter 1), when King Perión awaits Elisena alone in his bedchamber, and before they consummate their love, the expectant lover has a disturbing dream. He imagines that some unrecognizable person slips into his room, takes his heart from his body, and throws it into a river, saying that Perión has another heart which will also be taken from him, although not by this person's wish. Perión is so upset and frightened that, when Elisena, led by Darioleta, arrives in the moonlight, he appears before them armed with sword and shield. Back in his kingdom (in Chapter 2), Perión is still worried about this dream, and makes three of his cleric-wisemen swear on the host to tell him what it was about. Although they, significantly, tell him that dreams are empty things, they go off to think about the matter. First one and then another tell Perión that the dream refers to attacks on his kingdom and the taking of a town or castle, but eventually the wisest of them, Ungán the Picard, sees the king alone and informs him that the dream refers to his love and its consummation with Elisena, to Amadís's being cast upon the sea, and to Galaor's later kidnapping by the giant. This satisfies Perión although he hopes that the prophecies do not come true. By this time, of course, Amadís has been dispatched in his ark, but the reader's interest is still unsatisfied about Galaor's fate.

Much later (in Chapter 31), Queen Brisena, having just discovered the loss of the mantle and the crown from her chest, reveals that she has had a dream in which a damsel asked her for the key of the chest from which she took both articles and then closed it; she then put on the crown and mantle and said that they would in five days belong to him who will reign in the land of him who now seeks to defend it, and to conquer others' lands, but she did not say who this is and then she disappeared. We also know that this is an example of Arcaláus's magic, and it is clear that the person referred to by the damsel is none other than Barsinán, the usurper of Lisuarte's kingdom.

Two further uses of the dream concern Amadís himself during his period of anguish and exile as a result of Oriana's letter. First (in Chapter 45), as he is still suffering from the initial shock, he recalls a dream he had the night before which, he now sees, heralded his present state of distress. In this dream he saw himself on horseback on a hill surrounded by many happy people, when a man came up and asked him to eat from a box; this food was most bitter and caused him to feel faint and let his horse lead him off, while the happy ones became very sad; Amadís then went off to a wild part of the wood where he met a friar who comforted him and spoke to him in an unintelligible language, at which he awaked. This dream, told with convincing and observed detail, is used again partly to underline what has just happened and to foretell events soon to come to pass.

Amadís's other dream occurs (in Chapter 48) just before he embarks for the Peña Pobre. He finds himself locked in a dark room when Mabilia and the Damsel of Denmark come to him with a ray of sunlight before them which dispels the darkness; they then take him by the hand and ask him to go out into a great palace where he sees Oriana surrounded by a great flame of fire, through which he passes without hurt, and he then takes her in his arms in the greenest and most beautiful garden imaginable.

A little later (in Chapter 51), Andalod the hermit interprets these dreams for him in reverse order; the dark room is Amadís's distress, the fire around Oriana is her great care for him, and the garden their great subsequent joy. The hermit here says that Amadís should not speak of such things as dreams but he still goes on to calm Amadís's distress of mind—we recall the earlier disinclination of Perión's three clerics—but as we know the interpretation of dreams can have a therapeutic effect. The first dream's meaning is as clear, and the hermit adds that the people surrounding Amadís are his subjects on the Ínsola Firme who are glad and sad for him in turn—it will be recalled that he received Oriana's letter on the island.

Finally, Mabilia, Oriana's damsel, has a dream (in Chapter 77), during the period when Queen Sardamira has come as one of El Patín's emissaries for Oriana, and has been telling them about the deeds in Bohemia of a knight who, Oriana suspects, is Amadís. This dream again concerns a locked room from which Mabilia, Oriana, and the others hear frightening noises outside, until a knight breaks in, asks for Oriana, and takes her and the others outside and into a wonderful tower, where he tells them not to be afraid. Oriana needs no one to interpret this for her and she thanks Mabilia and prays God to send Amadís, now absent from her for several years, in order to save them or to let him and them die together.

Again this natural phenomenon contributes to the characters' development in the story and also whets the reader's appetite for what is to come. The dream as used in the *Amadís*, it can be seen, is presented with psychological insight and truth to experience, while, like other sections of the contents of the story, it also acts as a structural device.

CHAPTER 7

Description, Background, Geography, and Language

THIS chapter will attempt to look at four other features of the *Amadís*, three of which like others inform the whole narrative, while the fourth one forms its covering and gives it its external appearance. Description is a recurring element often displaying a vivid sense of realism and keenly observed detail. The geography of the *Amadís* is another kind of framework within which the many ingredients are held, while the language deserves at least a final if brief mention even for nonspecialist readers of this monograph. Once more it will not be possible to avoid a certain amount of repetition, since these elements have all contributed to our study of the *Amadís* in the preceding chapters. Still, it is thought necessary to examine, separately and, appropriately, at the end, those features which make up the common currency of our story and which are especially employed to set out and to hold together the other contents as well as to bring them into relief.

I *Description*

Realism is, of course, not always a subject easy to define, and it would be impertinent to attempt to do so here other than to suggest the workaday meaning which refers to that vividness which gives supporting and convincing detail to actions and scenes of any kind. The subject matter of the *Amadís* is remote from that of the modern novel, partly because it reflects a society long since defunct and also because it reflects only part of that society. This chapter will, however, try to show that the portrayal is carried out, as we have already seen, with recurrent attention to psychological truth and to exactness of description. The *Amadís* brings alive both the strange and the familiar, both the real and the fantastic.

141

The innumerable cases of individual combat and other encounters take place in surroundings that are often illuminated, even if briefly, by a little picture or a sudden detail which fixes the action sharply in the reader's memory. This use of realism to deepen the narrative can run from the unblinking and the shocking to the idyllic and the pastoral. Scenes of combat, like certain structural devices and references to religion, abound in our romance, and the use of them as illustrations of realism and description must therefore be very selective. They mark most of the climaxes of the action, beginning with the first adventure of King Perión and ending with the last full one of Amadís. Their repetitiveness can also be said to demonstrate the novel's length and variety.

In one of our hero's first encounters, while he is still known as the Donzel del Mar (in Chapter 4), the author describes his prowess in attacking his (unnamed) treacherous enemy in these stark terms:

he struck him so hard on his shield that he went through, and through the arm holding it, and brought him and his horse to the ground with such force that the knight broke his shoulder and, with the fall, the horse one of its legs . . . he then went for the other two [there were three opponents] and they for him, and the Youth struck one of them on top of his shield and severed it down to the armhold and reached his shoulder, so that its point cut into his flesh and bones; as for the other he struck him with such strength on the head that he made him throw his arms around his horse's neck. (I, 47–48)

This encounter is typical of many, with its details of the bloodiness and brutality of hand-to-hand combat. Thus the most common kind of episode in the *Amadís* is accompanied by clear attention to its reality, although it will also have been noted that the fearsome details of the hero's skill and strength are used to create his presentation as a superman.

Later (in Chapter 13) we are given a much livelier and fuller account (again quite typical) of Amadís and the proud and arrogant Dardán fighting it out to the finish, over three pages of text, in full view of Lisuarte and a great company of knights; and, as it turns out, in the presence of his beloved Oriana. First they fight, as happened in real jousts, on horseback with lance and then sword:

And Dardán and Amadís moved against each other from afar, and their horses were so speedy and swift, and they struck each other with such force and so wildly that all their weapons missed their mark, but neither was wounded, although their lances were split, and they then ran their horses against each other and hit their shields together so strongly that it was a wonder to see. Dardán went down from this first joust but he fell so luckily that he kept his reins in his hands and Amadís passed by and Dardán then got up quickly. They then struck each other on top of their helmets of fine steel, so that everyone thought their heads were alight, because of the great fire that came from them, while they let fall many fragments and pieces of mail, from their coats of armor and other weapons, and many chips from their shields. Amadís, seeing that the knight was taking so long to give in, began to rain great and hard blows on him. (I, 117–118)

This running battle (not unlike fights in certain modern films) goes on, after some interruption, when it looked as if one or the other had the upper hand:

Then without more delay they got down from their horses and each one took what was left of his shield, and with great fearlessness they went for each other, and struck each other much more savagely than before, so that it was a wonder to watch. But the strange knight [i.e., Amadís] had by far the advantage, as he could more easily get at the other; he struck him very frequently with very great blows, not letting him have any rest, as he saw he must do, and often he made him turn now one way now the other, and sometimes he brought him to his knees. Thus the strange knight had Dardán completely at his mercy, and Dardán tried more to save himself from the blows than to strike, and went out toward the palace of the queen and her ladies, while everyone said that he would die if he carried on fighting. (I, 119)

In fact, after a further encounter, Amadís leaves the field and Dardán kills first his beloved and then himself, bringing to an end an episode of dramatic violence and vivid movement.

There are, of course, several vivid examples in the *Amadís* of multiple combat or full-scale battle, which are treated with equal attention to the details of brutality. Thus, in the great battle fought by Amadís and his companions for Briolanja against Abíseos and his host (in Chapter 42):

Darasión had a chance to drive his sword through Amadís's horse's belly, and it began to flee with Amadís, who could not hold it, although he pulled in the reins so hard that they came away in his hand; when he saw that the horse would take him out of the field, he hit it with his sword so hard between the ears that he divided its head in two and it fell dead. . . . Then Agrajes hit Darasión such a blow with his sword on the helmet that he could not pull it out and Darasión went on with it in his helmet and began to strike Amadís great blows with his. . . . Darasión then threw his sword away and took him tightly in his arms, and, as they pulled at each other, they left their saddles and fell to the ground. (I, 340–341)

Of the many cases of this kind of realism to be found in the *Amadís*, two or three more will suffice. First, there is the case, again to be encountered elsewhere in the novel, of the devilish monster Andandona, the female giant who, when Amadís and his friends are on their way back to Gaul (in Chapter 65), tries to kill them all, but who in her fury falls into the sea, although not before wounding Bruneo in the leg. Then this lively scene occurs:

then they saw her emerge, swimming so strongly it astonished them, and they began to shoot at her with bows and arrows, but she ducked under the water until she got safely to the shore. As she climbed onto the land, Amadís and Cildadán each struck her with an arrow in the shoulder, but as she left the sea she took to flight through the dense thickets; King Cildadán, as he saw her with arrows stuck into her, could not help laughing. They then went to Don Bruneo and, stanching his wounds, they put him to bed. (II, 683–684)

The macabre humor of this gruesome situation has been commented on in an earlier chapter. Gandalín, Amadís's squire, finishes off Andandona by cutting off her head (in Chapter 68).

We have seen how Amadís's encounter with the Endriago (in Chapter 73) forms a special climax in our hero's career. This is true too for the use of horrific detail: as Amadís succeeds, it would seem, according to the text, with God's help, in wounding the monster fatally, it has still enough strength to hurt him most cruelly:

But the Endriago, when he saw him so close, threw his arms around him, and with his very strong and sharp claws broke all his shoulder armor, and tore his flesh and broke his bones until he reached his entrails (III, 802).

When the Endriago dies immediately afterward, these fearful wounds cause Amadís also to fall as one dead, but eventually the priest-physician Elisabad is brought to cure him (and there are a good many other examples in the novel of realism dealing with the results or aftermath of violence):

and looking at his wounds he saw that all the injury was to his flesh and his bones, and that it had not touched his entrails. He then had greater hope of curing him, and he set his bones and ribs, and sewed up his flesh and put on it such balms and so bound up all his body, that he stanched his blood and stopped his breath from emerging through his wounds. Then the knight gained more consciousness and more strength, so that he was able to speak. (III, 803–804)

The last example of realism in portraying violence can appropriately be taken from the savage battle in the streets of Lubaina (in Chapter 117), as Arcaláus and his host treacherously attack Lisuarte and his men; these scenes recall contemporary chronicles to which, as has been suggested, the *Amadís* owes something: "When King Lisuarte and those knights his servants found themselves finished, since they thought it worse to be taken prisoner than to be killed, you couldn't imagine the great wonders they there performed and the hard blows they delivered, for their enemies could not reach them, but with the strength of their lances they forced them back" (IV, 1155).

Help, as we know, comes just in time: "and when he [Amadís] reached the town, he saw people inside and some others outside, and he then went around it once and they struck and killed all they could reach. . . . And when they found people out of control and without fear, they killed many of them but others shut themselves up from them in the houses" (IV, 1156–1157).

Then Amadís, after the long and unhappy separation, at last meets King Lisuarte, in this gory but moving scene: "And he saw the king standing close to him, and he turned around. And when he went closer he looked at the king and he had all his flesh torn to pieces and covered with the blood from his wounds, and he took great pity to see him thus. . . . And when he went closer still, he dismounted and went toward him and got down on his knees and made to kiss his hands" (IV, 1158).

These recurring scenes of brutal violence and of carnage make up a very significant part of the ordinary stuff of the narrative of the *Amadís*, and they occur with rather more regularity and greater detail than in the *Sergas* or such other late Spanish versions of the Vulgate Breton material as the *Baladro del sabio Merlín* or the *Tristán de Leonís*. Even if the whole setting of the *Tirant* (the *Amadís*'s famous Hispanic contemporary in chivalric prose fiction) is more recognizably in the real world and its general use of realism therefore the greater, nevertheless the basic subject matter of our romance shows a clear and continuous awareness of the brute reality of the society of knights and of jousting on which it draws, and this, as we have noticed, extends to the compelling fantasy of such creations as Andandona, the Endriago, and Urganda's serpent-ship.

II *Background*

An altogether different use of vivid detail for background description is to be found in the profusion of scenes from nature and of men's dwellings of one kind and another. Many of these scenes are brief, but they all have their own suggestiveness for the main story.

The frequent idyllic vignettes can serve different kinds of situations. Thus (in Chapter 8) Amadís, as the Donzel del Mar, recalls his absent beloved when he becomes aware of nature's beauty, described here, it is true, in a very conventional manner: "This was in the month of April, and entering a wood he heard the birds sing and saw flowers on all sides" (I, 67).

Among many little descriptions of palaces, fortresses and castles, there is, for example, the more carefully observed scene which meets Amadís's eyes at nighttime (in Chapter 13), again early in his career: "Then leaving the road he went on until he reached a fine fortress in one of the towers of which there appeared at the windows those lights belonging to candles, and he heard men's and women's voices as if they were singing" (I, 108).

Oriana's private abode, the Castle of Miraflores, itself an evocative name, is described (in Chapter 53) in some detail, since it is after all the scene of great joy and grief for our hero and heroine, and the birthplace of their son:

This castle was two leagues from London; it was small but was the most pleasant dwelling in all that land, for its position was in a wood at one end of the mountain and it was surrounded by orchards with many fruits and other groves in which there were little plants and flowers of many kinds. It was built marvelously well, and inside were halls and chambers of rich design, and in the courtyards many fountains of very delicious water overhung by trees which had fruit and flowers all the year round. . . . (II, 432)

This, of course, in its details, recalls many such descriptions of bowers of bliss in a whole succession of medieval romances, and it also looks forward to the variety of similar scenes in the pastoral novel, itself also a Spanish product, and in much narrative verse and drama.

As we have said, the *Amadís* is a book of the open spaces rather than of the city or town—even Constantinople is described in general and not especially evocative detail. We have for instance seen how it contains frequent scenes of the hunt. It is therefore not surprising that it should also present quite a few sea scenes. These have been seen in Urganda's visits in her serpent-ship, and they also play a part in Amadís's wanderings in eastern Europe. Thus, when on his way from Rumania to the Greek court, and just before he meets and defeats the Endriago, Amadís and his companions run into a savage storm:

As the Knight of the Green Sword and his companions sailed over the sea with a very good wind, it suddenly changed round, as often happens, and the sea became so stormy, and went so far beyond all measure, that neither the strength of the ship, which was great, nor the skill of the sailors, was able to put up enough resistance to prevent it from being often in danger of foundering. The rain was so heavy and the winds so powerful, and the sky so dark, that everyone greatly despaired for their lives as being beyond remedy. . . . Often the ship, both by day and night, filled up with water on them, so that they had no rest nor could they eat or sleep. . . . (III, 792)

The Ínsola Firme is, it will be recalled, described at some length (in the first, unnumbered, chapter of Book II). It too contains details reminiscent of combat and also of the scenes of palaces and gardens found elsewhere in the book. The realistic account of this rather mixed area of reality and fantasy clearly provides much of the interest it has as a haven and an idyllic retreat. Much later in the *Amadís* (in Chapter 84), when our hero, having defeated Salustanquidio in the sea battle—also described at some length—brings his beloved in triumph to his island, she and her ladies are lodged in Apolidón's special apartments in a tower. The significance of this first use of the Ínsola Firme as a retreat for Amadís and Oriana is to be seen in the rather unusual detail with which these apartments are now described, again recalling the lovers' bower of bliss (an extract will suffice):

this tower was placed in the midst of an orchard surrounded by a high wall of very beautiful stone and bitumen, and it was for its trees and other plants of all kinds and its springs of very sweet water the most beautiful orchard that ever was seen. This garden also had some rich arcades attached to the wall and closed in with golden nets from which one could see all the greenery, and along these arcades one could go right around without being able to emerge except through certain doors. The floor was flagged with stones as white as crystal and others bright red like rubies, which Apolidón had ordered to be brought from certain islands to the East. On the four sides of the tower there came down from the high mountain four streams which surrounded it; these were carried by metal pipes and water ran from them at such a height through some pillars of golden copper and through the mouths of animal figures that from the first windows one could use the water, which was collected in some round troughs mounted on the pillars. The whole orchard was watered by these four streams. (IV, 968)

The text of the *Amadís* provides further striking examples of description used for background effect and other narrative purposes, that is, in addition to those examined above. Thus, Macandón's enchanted sword and headdress (in Chapter 56), and Urganda's ship (in Chapter 60), both of which cases we have looked at under other headings. A touchingly realistic account is given of Oriana's delivery and of Esplandián's birth (in Chapter 66), the attire and retinue of Queen Grasinda are colorfully described, (in Chapter 85), and a little pen portrait of Perión as the venerable king and military leader is given (in Chapter 107) just before the great battle with Lisuarte. It is also noticeable that Book IV contains less variety of detail of the general descriptive kind than the other three books. This is perhaps what one might expect from a section of the story which is more concerned with the action leading to the final climax.

A curiously effective kind of background detail is that which concerns the use of different languages among the many characters of the *Amadís*. This feature is found in only a few cases but they can be said to underline the novel's extensive geographical coverage (which will be considered below). For example, in the earlier part of the story (in Chapter 49), Oriana, in despair at having caused Amadís's departure through her jealousy, decides to send the Damsel of Denmark to Scotland, since she believes that her lover would have returned to the home of Gandales, who had rescued and reared him. Gandales, on meeting the damsel, and as the text puts it, "vio en su lenguaje que era stranjera" ("saw in her language that she was a foreigner"), nevertheless receives her warmly since she comes from Oriana. Later (in Chapter 72) we get a more illuminating case: Amadís, after leaving the king of Bohemia, is approached on the road by Grasinda's damsel, who addresses him; Amadís, we are told, "although the damsel's language was German, understood her at once very well, since he always tried to learn the languages of wherever he went" (III, 783). This interesting reference certainly adds something to our impression of Amadís as he wanders abroad and offers his sword to other people.

Not long afterward (in Chapter 78), when Amadís has brought Princess Grasinda to Lisuarte's court, they summon his major-domo's daughter, Grinfesa, who is described as a good person and with her own skills, and who "sabía ya quanto del lenguaje francés" ("already knew quite a lot of French"), which language, we are also told, King Lisuarte understood. This girl was given a Latin statement to take to Lisuarte and his queen, and she was also requested not to speak or reply in any language other than French as long as she remained with Amadís and Grasinda. Thus the simple use of a language for interpretation provides its own credibility to the narrative. Soon after this (in Chapter 79), Amadís, having beaten the arrogant Roman Gradamor, pretends that, as the Greek Knight, he does not understand his language, and thus he does not listen to his appeal for mercy. Then again (in Chapter 80), the old knight Grumedán, on whose loyalty to Lisuarte we have commented above, receives a sword from Amadís (as the Greek Knight) and from the hands of Grasinda's damsel, who for the occasion is said to address Grumedán "por el lenguaje francés" ("through the French language"). Thus we have two echoes of its early use as an international language, as it were!

As a result of Amadís's experiences in eastern Europe we get a couple of more interesting references to his knowledge of the Greek language. First, when at last he reaches the Greek court at Constantinople (in Chapter 74), he kneels before the empress offering his services to her and her ladies. He then adds that, if in this he does not fully succeed, she should, "since this language is strange to me, be pleased to pardon me, for it is but a very little time since I have learned it from Master Elisabad" (III, 814). This confirms Amadís's linguistic ability and readily suggests his very credible humility in strange and rather awesome surroundings. As Amadís is about to set out for home with Princess Grasinda, he emphasizes the

rigors of the journey by telling her (in Chapter 75) that she will have
to travel through many foreign or strange lands and meet peoples of
divers languages.

Another brief reference, with its own significance, to the Greek
language, comes (in Chapter 78) when Lisuarte is warned by still
another person, his uncle Count Argamón, of the dire results of his
forced marriage of Oriana to El Patín and the coming challenge to
the Romans by the Greek Knight (Amadís) and others. Lisuarte then
begs Argamón to stay for the challenges because "mejor que hombre
de mi tierra entendéys el lenguaje griego, según el tiempo que en
Grecia moraste" ("better than any man in my land you understand
the Greek language, because of the time you have dwelt in
Greece"). Indeed (in the following Chapter 79), Argamón soon puts
his special knowledge to use when, as the challenge begins, Amadís,
in speaking Greek, explains to Lisuarte why he is there, and this is
then interpreted by Argamón, saying that it is Amadís's intention to
reduce the Romans' pride. Again (in the same chapter) Argamón has
another chance by once more speaking Greek to intervene for
Lisuarte and save Salustanquidio's head after Amadís has downed
him in the challenges. Thus Amadís not only used Greek as a simple
means of communication but also as a natural aid to his disguise
when he arrives at Lisuarte's court with Grasinda. We recall that
later in the same Chapter 79 he pretends not to understand what a
Roman is saying.

Finally, and as if to sum up Amadís's linguistic gifts (and those of
his teacher), there is a striking reference in one of the last chapters
of the novel, when, in the midst of his last adventure, on the Peña
de la Donzella Encantadora (in Chapter 133), he is able to put his
knowledge to further practical use and to translate, for Grasandor
and himself, the mysterious inscription on the effigy's tablet. The
author comments thus: "Amadís began to read it, for in the period
when he traveled through Greece he learned quite a lot of its
language and alphabet, and much of this Master Elisabad had taught
him when they sailed the sea, and he also taught him the language of
Germany and other lands, for he knew them very well, as one who
was wise in all the arts and had traveled through many provinces"
(IV, 1293). This reference to German and the other one above
concerning Grasinda's damsel would seem to reflect its use in central Europe in the days of the Holy Roman Empire.[1]

III   *The Geography of the* Amadís

The geography of the *Amadís*, an area of the novel of which the references to different languages are, as suggested above, an indirect reflection, has been commented on by more than one critic, including Miss Williams, Menéndez y Pelayo, E. B. Place, and P. Bohigas. The wide use of geographical names (real or imaginary) also recalls the rich variety of personal names reviewed in our Chapter 5. Indeed, one of the charms of the *Amadís* is undoubtedly the sensation it gives of taking place amid a much-populated world that stretches from one land into others. This extensive coverage, of course, is again to be found in more than one other medieval romance—one recalls the Alexander and the Trojan tales—and it is also an important feature in the great Italian poems of the period of the *Amadís*, namely, the *Orlando innamorato* and the *Orlando furioso*.

The coexistence of the real world and that of enchantment has already been noted. It is paralleled by the fusion of real places and those from fantasy (one must again exclude names from the ancient world). Both taken together might be said to add up to a simple definition of what the *Amadís* is about. This consistent intermingling of the real and the imagined is an appealing characteristic of much early modern European fiction (and in fact goes back as far as the *Odyssey*), and we have tried to analyze some of the resulting mixture above.

As for the real places, the action of the *Amadís*, as we know, takes place chiefly in Great Britain, the kingdom of Lisuarte, who is served by Amadís and many other knights and who can also claim the help and loyalty of other kings and lords. Scotland also comes into the picture at an early stage as the home of the young Amadís and the temporary abode of Oriana. Ireland is the kingdom of Abiés, Amadís's early enemy, and of Quadragante, his later friend. Gaul, that little ill-defined kingdom near to Brittany, is, of course, the land of King Perión and of our hero, who takes his name from it. Little Britain (Brittany) also appears early on, North Wales (Norgales) is mentioned as the kingdom of Arbán, Amadís's ally, and Cornwall occurs once. Of other neighboring lands and places, Spain is mentioned just a few times and as the kingdom of Ladasán and of his son Brián de Monjaste; Granada, Saragossa, Medina del Campo, and Portugal each appear once; Germany, a vague concept then, occurs a few times, but Rome, its emperor and capital city, as well as its rulers and followers, play quite an important role in the novel; Sardinia often appears in the title of its queen, Sardamira; Zeeland gets a few passing references, as do Denmark, Queen Brisena's home, and home of Oriana's faithful damsel of this name, Norway and Sweden. Other places in western Europe mentioned only once, but, however, making their own small contributions to the total reality of our romance, are Burgundy, Lombardy, Normandy (seen as opposite the British port of Tagades), Calabria, the Mediterranean, and the Ocean Sea (Atlantic).

Eastern Europe, visited for long by Amadís, is an important region in the later part of the novel, and thus we meet with Bohemia, Rumania—Dacia, its older name, is also that of a royal family—and Greece and its great capital city, Constantinople. These latter, of course, are the abodes of the emperor and empress, of Grasinda, Leonorina, and others. It has been suggested above that the presence of Greece in the *Amadís* reflects the contemporary preoccupation with the Turks and their advance into Europe; certainly the resulting struggle forms part of the action of the *Sergas* and the *Tirant*. Further east, India is mentioned once and Tartary twice (the *Orlando furioso* goes further east to China). The much visited regions of the West also have their towns, that is, apart from the Spanish ones and the imperial city mentioned above: thus, for England, we have Arundel, Bristol, London, Gloucester, Gravesend, Windsor, and Winchester, although several others belong to the realm of fantasy or are unidentifiable.

Imaginary place-names indeed claim at least as much attention as those of the geography of history, and, as we know, they include certain regions of central importance to the *Amadís*, and are also associated with the whole range of its characters. Thus we have Sansueña, kingdom of the usurper Barsinán (this place, with much currency in the Hispanic tradition, stood for legendary places and also for Pamplona and Saragossa); Suesa, kingdom of Lancino; Serolís, kingdom of Adroid, father of the damsel Aldeva; and the neighboring Sobradisa, kingdom of Queen Briolanja. Arabia, and its towns, although a real place, is used as the abode of King Arábigo, ally of Arcaláus.

The true sense of fictional geography, however, is created and maintained by the use of the distinctive abode of the *Amadís*, namely, the island. The island has, of course, for long played a significant role in literature, standing as a haven and a place of peril, of enchantment and protection, of delights and horrors. Thus its uses by Homer and others in the ancient world, by medieval romance, by Montalvo's Italian contemporaries, Boiardo and Ariosto, and, in the period after our romance, by Tasso, Camoens, and Shakespeare, and much later, by Defoe and R. L. Stevenson. Cervantes, it will be recalled, made his own ironic contribution to this fascinating tradition! In the *Amadís* this geographical feature usually goes under the semi-Latinized form "Ínsola." Of these the most important is, of course, the Ínsola Firme, often referred to above. It represents a retreat and the abode reserved for the good and the brave. We are told that it is situated close to the mainland (which one is not stated), but it is visited by many others, including Arcaláus, apart from Amadís and his companions. Its exact position *vis-à-vis* the other main center of action, namely, Great Britain, is not made clear, but one feels it should be close enough, since the final battles move from one to the other, and Amadís and his company go to the island after sailing home via Spain and the open sea, while others arrive at the Ínsola Firme from Gaul and Great Britain, without any reference being made to a lengthy journey. At the same time, the island has been the home of the two Greeks, Apolidón and Grimanesa. The former reached it by way of Rome, where he met his beloved, and by ship, and they left it eventually by ship to return together to Greece. The impression is thus left that the Ínsola Firme is somewhere in the West. It can be seen that the chief island in the *Amadís* illustrates well how this older kind of romance moves according to its own rules of fictional probability.

Of the other islands, some far off, some, it would seem, close enough, the mysterious Ínsola no Fallada or Dudada is, as we have seen, appropriately the abode of Urganda la Desconocida. Others belong to the opponents of Amadís and Lisuarte and, as noted above, are also the homes of giants, thus symbolizing places of hostility. We also recall how at one point (in Chapter 67) Arcaláus was stirring up the lords of the islands under Arábigo's leadership. This last is himself king of the Ínsola de las Landas, possibly recalling the French Landes, while he retreats to one of the latter, the Ínsola de Liconia (recalling an ancient name), and he uses the Ínsola Leonida—not far, it would seem, from Great Britain—as a rallying point prior to his first attack on Lisuarte (in Chapter 68). The Ínsola

Sagitaria is, as the name indicates, the abode of giant bowmen, allies of Arcaláus and Arábigo, as was the king of the Profunda Ínsola (Deep Island); the ínsola de la Torre Bermeja (Island of the Red Tower) belonged to the giant Balán, who, we recall, mended his ways, while the Ínsola Triste was the home of the giant Madarque, also finally tamed. Most suitably, the hideout of the worst of all enemies, the Endriago, is called the Ínsola del Diablo, that is, one of the islands of Rumania visited by Amadís, which, once the monster was killed, Amadís suggested might be renamed the Island of St. Mary, now to be repopulated (we recall too that the Ínsola Firme had been "cleansed" by Apolidón). The Ínsola de Mongaça was to be the joint home of Madasima and her new husband Galvanes, about whom Amadís and Lisuarte had a rather pointless dispute, and in which was situated the Lago Ferviente (Boiling Lake), abode of Gromadaça, wife of the giant Famongomadán. The Ínsola del Infante belonged to King Cildadán and was visited by Amadís on his way to wage war with Balán, and finally the Ínsolas Luengas (Long Islands) are said to have belonged to Galeote, a friend of Lancelot of the Lake.

As well as such a fictionally convenient place as an island (of which a good many in any case exist off the coasts of the British Isles), there are in the *Amadís* other specifically named features, isolated and small. Thus the Peña Pobre (Poor Peak) whither Amadís retired as the hermit Beltenebrós, and the Peña de Galtares, taken from the good giant Gandalás by the bad one Albadán. There are also some castles, like Gantasi of the other Madasima, the Castillo del Gran Rosal (of the Great Rosebush), where Cildadán freed Celinda and made love to her, and the Castillo de la Calzada (of the Causeway), where Amadís dubbed his brother Galaor a knight in the presence of Urganda. Towers are another feature of the landscape of the romance if not strictly of its geography: thus, the Torre Bermeja, not to be confused with the island of the same name, of the giant Madanfabul, and the Torre de la Ribera (of the Riverbank), abode of a tyrant. One could go further and recall even smaller features such as fountains, of which some five, with rural names, are referred to as meeting places, and three forests or woods which recall certain hazardous encounters. Castles, peaks, fountains, and woods belong, of course, to the common currency of our romance and thus do not really merit special attention.

In conclusion, one should recall the limits of the geography of history and the extent to which imaginative regions invade the scene and dominate parts of the story. The reader is early introduced to a world centered on Great Britain but which eventually stretches as far as Greece, and it should again be said that this was a European rather than a Hispanic panorama. Geographical reality is made to impinge on us when we are told of specific journeys. Thus it takes eight days from Sansueña to Great Britain, or twenty from Great Britain to Sansueña; also, one goes by sea from Great Britain to Gaul or Gaul to Great Britain, as one does from Constantinople to Great Britain, passing the coast of Spain, and one also sails from Great Britain to Rome. Much if not all of this going to and fro occurs in Book IV and concerns the preparations for the last great battles in the Ínsola Firme and Great Britain. Once again it should be stated that this section of the novel may well show the imprint of Montalvo rather than of his predecessor. Amadís when on his way through central and eastern Europe goes on horseback, although he too takes ship more than once when there. Also, there are, as we know, both battles and sea storms, which keep the presence of the land as well as of the water before us.

This reasonably precise and identifiable area within which much of the action of the *Amadís* develops also very naturally and almost casually incorporates within it the realm of fantasy. Many of the place-names, as of the personal names, have been shown to be of Breton origin and some also come from other sources such as the Trojan cycle. This in itself would add a note of familiarity for the first generations of readers to whom the earlier material of romance would be well known and for whom the deliberate mixing of the historical and the imaginative in their favorite kind of literature would be quite acceptable. As pointed out before, the appeal of the *Amadís* would owe something to the fact that it was a fresh variation of material well established in the taste and fashions of the age.

It is hoped that another examination of distinct areas of our romance will have helped to illuminate the whole and have illustrated its variety. In particular, it will have been seen once more how the *Amadís* has its being in open country as well as in many countries.

IV *The Language*

The language of the *Amadís*, like that of any serious work of literature, deserves some separate attention even in a general study of the romance. Much work, however, still remains to be done on this important aspect of the *Amadís*, since only very short studies of it have so far been published. It should also be stated that the repeated (but unsubstantiated) assertions about the Portuguese origins of the romance and the (also unproved) existence of a Portuguese manuscript version have led some modern critics to claim that the language of our only known version, the Spanish one, shows clear signs of Portuguese forms. Thus Rodrigues Lapa points to the language of the 1955 fragments for evidence of this. On the other hand, his compatriot Costa Marques sees nothing distinctly Portuguese in the language of the *Amadís*. Others who have made studies of its language support this latter view.

The known history of the *Amadís* from the mid-1300s up to the first edition of 1508 plus the scanty manuscript evidence of an earlier text are reasons why the linguistic study of our romance should proceed with caution. The long period of unbroken popularity of the *Amadís* would, like that of other romances and long narratives, seem to indicate that the text as it has been preserved contains archaic features. At the same time the known intervention of Montalvo as editor and continuator of inherited material should also mean that his contributions are written in a language more typical of the late 1400s. The recent work of three scholars confirms these assumptions.

Dr. Gili y Gaya, in his lecture mentioned in Chapter 3 above, makes several important points about our romance. First, he draws attention to the extraordinary modernity of its language: the great Spanish classics of the 1500s, with their knowledge of the *Amadís*, show the clear imprint of its vocabulary, which has also influenced colloquial Spanish; in particular, the *Amadís*'s development of the period or complex sentence and of prose rhythms led to their perfection in *Don Quixote*, as did the former's use of a quick economic narrative style. Dr. Gili y Gaya might have added that Montalvo and his predecessors showed more predilection for such Latinisms as putting the verb at the end of the sentence or the use of the subjunctive tense in nonhypothetical clauses.

Gili y Gaya further makes it clear that the archaism of the *Amadís*'s language cannot be pushed back beyond c. 1340 and that in any case it is much more pronounced in Book I than in II and III, and even less in IV, the last of which he sees as Montalvo's own addition. In addition to this interesting general statement, based on a detailed study which unfortunately has not appeared, Dr. Gili y Gaya firmly asserts that the text of the *Amadís* has no linguistic Portuguesisms, since its older forms of vocabulary and syntax can easily be found in other Spanish prose writers of the late 1300s and the 1400s. (The present writer's reading of the text also confirms this view.) He then makes a similar statement about French forms or Gallicisms, which, in his view, are fewer than in earlier romances in Spanish and are in any case often the loan words which came to several countries from France as part of the language of chivalry and heraldry. Finally, for Gili y Gaya, Montalvo's contributions such as moralistic comments and shortenings of the text can be identified with the help of this general linguistic picture of the romance.

When Dr. Rodríguez-Moñino in 1957 brought out the precious manuscript fragments, Dr. Rafael Lapesa, as indicated above, placed their language as that typical of northwestern Castile and as belonging to an older text now partly modernized and of the period c. 1420. Third, Dr. E. B. Place, in volume two of his edition, echoes the views of Lapesa about the fragments and also those of Gili y Gaya in finding fewer archaisms in Books III and IV. Place's approach is "negative" insofar as he tries to disprove the thesis that the *Amadís*'s language has Portuguese forms, and therefore his coverage of the subject is limited.

The claims that have been made in this monograph for the excellences of the *Amadís* clearly depend on the riches of its vocabulary and general style, and some of these latter will have been glimpsed in the extracts from the text provided for comments above. The novel's sustained stylistic flow, both for narration and description, most certainly constitutes one of its delights for the reader and also stands out as a distinct virtue in a very long text. It has also been seen that the novel's other material such as moralistic comments, soliloquies, and letters can, however, be written in a more rhetorical and Latinized manner. The changing nature of the subject matter and the different moods created in the narrative are on the whole successfully rendered by the corresponding linguistic variety. The language of our romance still presents a rich and fruitful field of research for the medievalist.[2]

Summation

As stated in the Preface, the main aim of this monograph has been to attempt an analysis of the form and the contents of the *Amadís*. This can be justified on at least two grounds. First, the novel as such, as distinct from its origins and history, has not been the subject of a really detailed examination. Second, the very sparse information available on the life of its last author rules out anything but a passing consideration of his biography. In any case, the inherited nature of the material of our romance means that Montalvo should be seen as the craftsman who recast and elaborated a work which over a long period belonged to Spanish society as a whole. The *Amadís* was thus in a true sense a public possession rather than one man's private creation. There is, however, no intention to decry the significance of Montalvo's contributions, even if these cannot always be clearly identified. Some attention has also been given to the literary and social background of Montalvo's age. Less coverage has been granted to the "question," although its relevance cannot be ignored. After all, the reputation acquired by a work of art becomes part of its meaning and import.

The structure of our romance has been examined in order to discover how its extensive material has been set out and variety thus necessarily introduced, by means of narrative devices and other related arrangements of the story, as well as through the multiplicity of its characters and of the places in which its action takes place. Also, separate attention has been given to the novel's ideological and psychological content, since, like much subsequent fiction, the *Amadís* reflects in its own way the values of the society for which it was intended. Thus the need has been felt to look in some detail at such key topics as religion, love, magic, good, and evil, and in this way also it is hoped that something of the book's riches has been suggested. Some examination has been made of the complementary feature of description in its different forms as an integral part of the overall style, and a few words have been said about the novel's language. The *Amadís* is, of course, above all a novel about chivalry and love, the first a public, the second a private, dedication. These are exemplified throughout by Amadís and Oriana, who symbolized the institutions and the beliefs of an older world. They also were to become idealized human types, with great nostalgic appeal, for the cultivated European during many generations.

Finally, it must again be said that without the *Amadís* we should not have had *Don Quixote*, and without the latter the modern novel would have been very different.

Notes and References

Chapter One

1. Useful and up-to-date accounts of some of the material covered in this chapter are contained in the following: A. D. Deyermond, *The Middle Ages: A literary History of Spain*, Vol. I (London: Ernest Benn Ltd., 1971); P. E. Russell, ed., *Spain: A Companion to Spanish Studies* (London: Methuen & Co. Ltd., 1973); especially Chap. 3 by R. B. Tate, Chap. 4 by J. H. Elliott, Chap. 6 by Ian Michael, and Chap. 8 by P. E. Russell. For the few recorded facts of Montalvo's life and other references in his works, see the definitive article of Narciso Alonso Cortés, *Revue Hispanique*, 81, Pt. I 1933, 434–42. For chivalry in fifteenth-century Spanish society, see the impressive little monograph by Martín de Riquer, *Caballeros andantes españoles* (Madrid: Espasa calpe, 1967), and, for early Spanish printing, P. Bohigas's readable account *El libro español* (Barcelona, 1962). Maxime Chevalier, in his helpful study *Sur le public du roman de chevalerie* (Talence: Institut d'Etudes Ibériques et Ibéro-américaines de l'Université de Bordeaux, 1968) provides evidence of the survival, well into the 1500s, of pageants and jousts, based this time on the *Amadís*, in both France and Spain. This activity, however, appears to have ended around 1600, when the interest in chivalric literature itself was showing clear signs of dying. This interest, which lasted a long time, as we know, was largely if not exclusively confined, to judge from Dr. Chevalier's researches, to members of the nobility. The latter, through reading the whole romance or those parts of it that made up the *Thrésor*—that is, its use as a manual of courtly behavior (for which see Chapter 3)—appear to have seen in it an idealized image of their own way of life and a nostalgic harking back to the age of chivalric adventure. A good general account of the field to which the *Amadís* belongs is John Steven's *Medieval Romance: Themes and Approaches* (London: Hutchinson, 1974).

Chapter Four

1. Miss G. S. Williams (see her monograph, *Revue Hispanique*, 21 [1909], esp. pp. 39–154) has made the most thorough analysis to date of the

Amadís and its likely sources. Reference should also be made again to the more recent work of María Rosa Lida de Malkiel on this important aspect of the romance (see *Romance Philology*, 6 [1952–53], 283–89).

2. See Frida Weber de Kurlat, "Estructura novelesca del *Amadís de Gaula*," *Revista de literaturas modernas*, 5 (1967), 29–54. A more recent monograph by Armando Durán, *Estructura y técnicas de la novela sentimental y caballeresca* (Madrid: Gredos, 1973), refers to the structure of the *Amadís* (see especially pp. 100–11 and 154–61): after a summary of the important scholarship of this century concerning the primitive form of the work and Montalvo's changes, Dr. Durán analyzes the *Amadís* largely in terms of the hero's identity and of his love for Oriana; he finds that the early resolution of these two matters renders much of the novel weak and lacking in interest, while he also holds that Esplandián is an unnecessary creation. The open-endedness of the *Amadís* is further contrasted to its disadvantage with the greater compactness and crescendo of tension in the *Tirant lo blanc*. A passing reference (but with no real illustration) is made to the use of interweaving (*entrelacement*) in the *Amadís*, largely for the adventures after the hero's recognition by his parents. This fresh but rather partisan view of the structure of our romance would certainly not be shared by many of its critics, including Dr. Weber and the writer of the present monograph.

3. See his "Form and Meaning in Medieval Romance," p. 13 (the Presidential Address, Modern Humanities Research Association, 1966), and *The Rise of Romance* (New York: Oxford; 1971), p. 76.

4. See F. Pierce, "L'allégorie poètique au XVIᵉ siècle: Son évolution et son traitement par Bernardo de Balbuena," *Bulletin Hispanique*, 51 (1950), 381–406; 52 (1951), 191–228. See also Maxime Chevalier (*Sur le public du roman de chevalrie*, pp. 18–19), who draws attention to the continuing practice of editors and authors of novels of chivalry in emphasizing their moral value.

5. The device of using letters and harangues goes back in literature to ancient times, although they had much currency in the Middle Ages. For a very useful analysis of their use and that of other rhetorical features of contemporary prose, see the introduction by Keith Whinnom to his edition of the works of Diego de San Pedro (*Obras completas*, Vol. II [Madrid: Clásicos Castalia, 1971], pp. 44–66). See also Keith Whinnom, *Diego de San Pedro* (New York: Twayne, 1974), Chaps. 5 and 7. An earlier critical work, now a classic, is Edmond Faral's *Les arts poètiques du XIIᵉ et du XIIIᵉ siècles* (Paris: Champion, 1923).

Chapter Five

1. Once again one must go to Miss Williams ("The Amadís Question," pp. 46–60), here for a full listing and a discussion of the geographical and personal names (including epithets or nicknames) in the *Amadís*. Many of them, or variations of them, can again be found in the Round Table liter-

ature, and it is worth noting, too, that, for the most part, the personal names do not recall Christian names but may be said to be unique, and thus at once identifiable with the characters concerned, even if they are of Celtic or Trojan origin. This uniqueness of names of characters can also be noted in the Catalan ascetic novel, the *Blanquerna*, of Ramon Llull (1233–1316), and, to a certain extent, in the later Catalan romance, the *Tirant lo blanc* (1490). The same is true in varying degrees of much medieval and early modern epic and romance, including the Italian long poems of Pulci, Boiardo, and Ariosto. On the other hand, our own hero's name has more than once been made a topic of discussion and attempts have been made to connect it with other fictional figures bearing similar names, and with St. Amadas and St. Amadeus (see Miss Williams, pp. 50–52). Both Miss Williams (pp. 58–59) and Menéndez y Palayo (*Orígenes de la novela*, p. 337) remind us that certain names do have an explicit French meaning: Arcalaus (Arc-à-l'eau), Briolanja (Brion l'ange), and Angriote de Estravaus (Andrieux des Travaux).

2. The *Amadís*, like other romances, includes several giants among the human fauna that fill its pages. They can be good or bad and all of them appear to symbolize strength, size, and often savagery. They also rule over islands and thus tend to live somewhat apart. Thus Galaor's captor, Gandalás (in Chapter 3), is seen as a *jayán*, or very large man, with armor to match, and as producing an effect of fright on all who saw him. He was not such an evildoer as other giants, however, but had a good temperament, although he was quick to anger; finally, he had populated his island with Christians. Another good one was Balán, son of Madanfabul, who is also described (in Chapter 128) as very much a Christian. Of the others, Famongomadán (in Chapter 55), whose beautiful daughter Madasima was to marry Galvanes, is described as frightening because of his stature and his armor; Madanfabul (in Chapter 58) is also seen as an example of anger and fierceness; Madarque (in Chapter 65) is likewise conceived as fierce and a great killer, and also dressed in huge, shining armor, although he is finally tamed; but his sister Andandona is much worse: not alone is she wild, but as ugly as the devil and a tamer of wild animals, whose skins she wears.

The most fearsome of all is, of course, the Endriago, whose name stands for a dragon or monster (in Chapter 73): the fruit of incest between father and daughter (they both killed the mother and then married), he had to pay for this double sin by carrying within him the devil himself. His appearance is both repulsive and unhuman: body and face are covered with hair and impenetrable scales; feet and legs are very thick and strong; from his shoulders spring wings that come down to his feet and are of black leather and cover him like a shield; the arms are like a lion's and again covered with scales; his hands are like an eagle's, with very strong claws; his two teeth jut out from his jaw a cubit in length; and the eyes are large, round, and red like hot coals and frighten people from afar (the actual features of his father's idols are combined in his body). This monster, who also killed its own parents, and lived on an island appropriately called Devil's Island, jumped and ran faster than any deer and needed little food or drink, but his greatest pleasure was killing men and animals. His defenses were smokelike flames from his nostrils, hoarse cries, and an evil and poisonous smell, and he made the earth tremble. Amadís killed this creature by skill rather than strength, but was himself grievously wounded in the process. One can readily see what the Endriago symbolizes and how Amadís's victory remains one of his most heroic achievements. This monster is not human and thus essentially different from the giants. All of them, however, partake to some extent of the wild man whose role in literature and art has been constant if changing. See *The Wild Man Within*, edited by Edward Dudley and M. F. Novak (University of Pittsburgh Press, 1972), which says nothing about the *Amadís*, but covers the subject up to the nineteenth century. It has also been studied by R. Bernheimer, in *Wild Men in the Middle Ages: A Study in Art, Sentiment and Demonology* (Cambridge, Mass.: Harvard University Press, 1952), which contains little on the Spanish field. See in addition A. D. Deyermond's useful article, "El hombre salvaje en la novela senti-mental," *Filología*, 10 (1964), 97–111, which also includes comments on the pastoral novel.

3. Maxime Chevalier (*Sur le public du roman de chevalerie*, p. 19) quotes with approval Menéndez y Pelayo's insistence on the respect shown in the *Amadís* for the institution of the monarchy, which is thus seen as a feature distinguishing it from earlier romances.

4. Much has, of course, been written on courtly love (see note 6 below), but reference may be made here to the particular aspect of it which con-cerns lachrymosity and lamentation, and which is the subject of an im-pressive analysis by P. Gallagher (see *Forum for Modern Language Studies*, 9 [1973], 192–99) of Garcilaso's First Eclogue.

5. For the brief account of the *Tirant*, see A. Terry, *Catalan Literature: A Literary History of Spain* (London: Ernest Benn Ltd., 1972), pp. 50–53; and also F. Pierce, "The role of sex in *Tirant lo blanc*," *Estudis romànics*, 10 (1962), 291–300.

6. The treatment of love in medieval literature is both greatly varied and very complex, and the *Amadís* reflects a long and established tradition. Nevertheless, as has been suggested above, the love of a knight in literature is not exactly the same as that of the so-called courtly lover, if only because triumph and achievement are the normal rewards of the former. Anything more than a brief reference here to love in medieval literature would be out of place, although some mention should be made of the broader dimensions of the subject. The church, the medical profession, and the poetic rhetoricians on love all had their viewpoints, reflecting sharp differences, as they related to such things as carnality, adultery, conjugal love, the conflict of passion and reason, misogyny, and feminism. There was the courtly

tradition and there was the popular tradition of love in verse, and these presented extremes of idealization and grossness; and there was, of course, the love of God. Often medieval literature treats love with high rhetorical evasiveness and great verbal play, although, as the *Amadís* shows, it can also be described with fresh naturalness.

Much difference of view now exists among critics about the meaning of "courtly love" (a nineteenth-century invention as a term), and there is a healthy tendency to see the whole subject anew and to try to relate it to our own freer and less inhibited analyses of the phenomenon in literature and elsewhere. The literature is vast, but a very stimulating review and revision is provided by Keith Whinnom (see first work quoted in note 5 to Chapter 4 above, 7–37); one should also recall the now classic study of C. S. Lewis, *The Allegory of Love* (London: Oxford University Press, 1936; reprinted, 1967), and the more recent challenge to traditional interpretation by P. Dronke, *Medieval Latin and the Rise of European Love Lyric* (New York: Oxford, 1965–66). Reference is again made to the perceptive study by P. Gallagher, in note 4 above.

Chapter Six

1. Magic is also a vast topic in both literature and the arts as well as in theology, the sciences, and medicine. No monograph exists for its role in literature as such, but the following can be consulted: Vol. IV (covering the fourteenth and fifteenth centuries) of Lynn Thorndike's standard work, *A History of Magic and Experimental Science* (New York: Columbia University Press, 1934); and P. E. Russell's study of magic in the *Celestina* (*Studia Philologica: Homenaje ofrecido a Dámaso Alonso* [Madrid: Gredos, 1963], III, 337–54). This latter is of special interest to readers of the *Amadís* since it deals with a famous contemporary work and also emphasizes the changing views on magic in the society which produced both works of literature. Mention should also be made of J. B. Avalle-Arce's revealing article "El arco de los leales amadores en el *Amadís*," *NRFH*, 6 (1952), 149–56, which reexamines sources (especially the Byzantine ones) and indicates the prevalence of this part of the magic island.

2. For a general coverage of the subject see *Critical Approaches to Medieval Literature*, edited by Dorothy Bethurum (New York: Columbia University Press, 1960).

Chapter Seven

1. The subject of this chapter too is a very large and complex one. The role of realism of one kind and another in literature and art goes back, of course, to earliest times, and is far from being a recent invention of the novel or the film, for example, although it could be held that our own age has had a peculiar preoccupation with its own forms of realism. Among many titles that could be quoted, the famous essay of the Dutch humanist

Jan Huizinga, "Renaissance and Realism" (see his *Men and Ideas* [New York: Meridian Books Inc., 1960], pp. 288–309), can be quoted as having special relevance for the literature of the period of the *Amadís*. References to different languages spoken by the characters are also found a couple of times in the earlier Spanish romance, the *Caballero Cifar* (c. 1300), although the languages are not named (see ed. by C. P. Wagner [Ann Arbor: University of Michigan Publications in Language and Literature, 5, 1929], pp. 177 and 386–87). This appears seldom in medieval literature and may indeed reflect the long coexistence in Spain of different cultures and their languages. There are, however, some few references to the phenomenon in the *Orlando furioso* (e.g., in Cantos V, IX and XXIII), although of a less precise kind than in the *Amadís*, and also in the Catalan novel *Curial e Güelfa*, of the earlier 1400s (see ed. of "Els nostres clàssics," Vol. 39–40 [Barcelona: Barcino, 1933] 167).

2. For the language of the *Amadís*, see the following: S. Gili y Gaya, *Amadís de Gaula* (Barcelona, 1956); A. Rodríguez-Moñino, ed., *El primer manuscrito del "Amadís de Gaula"* (Madrid, 1957); and E. B. Place, ed., *Amadís de Gaula*, II (Madrid, 1962), 585–97.

Selected Bibliography

PRIMARY SOURCES

BUENDÍA, FELICIDAD, ed. *Amadís de Gaula*, in *Libros de caballerías españoles*. Madrid: Aguilar, 1954, pp. 309–1049 (based on the edition of Louvain, 1551). Has a very sound introductory essay on medieval romance and on the *Amadís* in particular, with a list of its early editions.

CARDONA DE GISBERT, ÁNGELES, and JOAQUÍN RAFEL FONTANELS, eds. *Amadís de Gaula*. Barcelona: Bruguera, "Libro Clásico," 1969. Reproduces the 1508 edition, with modernized spelling but with many misprints. A good introductory essay and a very good bibliography and general index.

GAYANGOS, PASCUAL DE, ed. *Amadís de Gaula*, in "Biblioteca de Autores Españoles." 1st ed., 1857; reprinted Madrid: Hernando, 1925, XL, 1–402 (based on the edition of Venice, 1533). Preceded by an essay on the earlier romances, on the *Amadís* and its successors, and an exhaustive list of printed editions of books of chivalry. The same volume contains the *Sergas de Esplandián* (pp. 403–561), and a very useful index of names and topics from both novels.

PLACE, E. B., ed. *Amadís de Gaula*. Madrid: Consejo Superior de Investigaciones Científicas; I, 1959, enlarged, 1971; II, 1962; III, 1965; IV, 1969. Reprints of the edition of Saragossa, 1508. Vol. I contains a full account of the early editions, translations, and adaptations (especially the *Thrésor d'Amadís de Gaule*, of 1559); Vol. II contains linguistic notes on I and II and a bibliography; Vol. III reviews the question of the novel's primitive form, the characters and its geography, and has further linguistic notes; Vol. IV contains Montalvo's life and discusses his reworking of the *Amadís*, with further notes and an index of the whole novel. Each volume also lists errata from the 1508 edition. Dr. Place's edition must now be seen as the standard text, as making available, with few changes, that of the first known edition.

RODRÍGUEZ-MOÑINO, A., et al., eds. *El primer manuscrito del "Amadís de Gaula."* Madrid: Aguirre Torre, 1957. Reproduces the now famous four fragments (all from Book III), discovered in 1955. Accompanied by comments on the bibliographical history involved (A. R.–M.), the palaeography of the manuscript (A. Millares Carlo), and the language (R. Lapesa).

SOUTHEY, ROBERT, trans. *Amadís of Gaul* by Vasco Lobeira. 3 vols. London: John Russell Smith, a New Edition, 1872. It is based on the edition of Seville, 1547 (some use being made of the English version of 1618). Probably the only easily accessible early translation (even if it is somewhat abridged and with a very out-of-date preface). Very readable if a bit quaint and old-fashioned in style.

SOUTO, ARTURO, ed. *Amadís de Gaula.* Mexico City: Porrúa, "Sepan cuantos," 1969. Reproduces Gayangos text, with reference also to the edition of Medina del Campo, 1545, for doubtful readings, but gives only Book I in full, and then "the most important chapters" of II–IV. A good introductory essay with a useful historical table. Very suitable for undergraduate study.

A new translation into English has been undertaken by E. B. Place and H. C. Behm, of which Books I and II have appeared as one volume: *Amadís of Gaul* (Lexington: University of Kentucky Press. Studies in Romance Languages, 11, 1974).

SECONDARY SOURCES

ALONSO CORTÉS, NARCISO. "Montalvo, el del *Amadís,*" *Revue Hispanique,* 63; Pt. I (1933), 434–42. Gives the few known facts of his life.

AVALLE-ARCE, JUAN BAUTISTA. "El arco de los leales amadores en al *Amadís,*" *Nueva Revista de Filología Hispánica,* 6 (1952), 149–52. Reexamines sources and shows origin in Byzantine novel.

BOHIGAS BALAGUER, PEDRO, in *Historia general de las literaturas hispánicas.* Ed. G. Díaz Plaja. Barcelona: Barna, I, 1949; II, 1951. Very good up-to-date and comprehensive survey of the origins of the novels of chivalry (I, 519–41), of the late medieval romances in Spanish, drawing from epic and history (II, 187–200), and of the *Amadís* and its successors (II, 213–36). Very good bibliographies. Highly recommended.

CHEVALIER, MAXIME. *Sur le public du roman de chevalerie.* Talence: Institut d'Etudes Hispaniques et Ibéro-américaines, Université de Bordeaux, 1968. A short scholarly monograph showing that in fact it was the nobility who made the form their own.

COSTA MARQUES, F. *Amadis de Gaula.* Lisbon: Clássicos Portugueses, 1942. Translation and reduction of the Spanish text to nine chapters. Balanced introductory survey of the subject and the Portuguese case.

EISENBERG, D. "Who read the romances of chivalry?" *Kentucky Romance Quarterly,* 20 (1973), 209–233. Scholarly and well-argued survey of the subject also analyzed by Chevalier, and with similar conclusions.

————. "*Don Quijote* and the Romances of Chivalry: The Need for a Reexamination." *Hispanic Review*, 41 (1973), 511–23. A critical revision of an important aspect of the fame of the romances.

ENTWISTLE, W. J. *The Arthurian Legend in the Literature of the Spanish Peninsula*. London: Dent, 1925. A classic survey, with much new information, and a critical summary of the "question."

GILI Y GAYA, SAMUEL. "Las Sergas de Esplandián como crítica de la caballería bretona." *Boletín de la Biblioteca Menéndez y Pelayo*, 22 (1947), 103–11. A valuable study of Esplandián as a Christian knight and a new Galahad.

————. *Amadís de Gaula*. Barcelona: Facultad de Filosofia y Letras, 1956, p. 26. One of the few serious studies of the novel's language and style and of their influence.

JAMESON, A. K. "Was There a French Original of the 'Amadís de Gaula'?" *Modern Language Review*, 28 (1933), 176–93. An ingenious but unprovable version of an old thesis.

LE GENTIL, P. "Pour l'interpretation de l'*Amadís*," In *Mélanges à la memoire de Jean Sarrailh*. Paris: Centre de Recherches de l'Institut d'Etudes Hispaniques, 1966, II, 47–54. Good study of why the *Amadís* appealed to its age.

LIDA DE MALKIEL, MARÍA ROSA. "El desenlace del *Amadís* primitivo." *Romance Philology*, 6 (1952–53), 283–89. Relatively short but very important critical revision of the shape of the early novel and its sources.

————. "Arthurian Literature in Spain and Portugal." In *Arthurian Literature in the Middle Ages: A Collaborative Study*. Ed. R. S. Loomis. Oxford: Clarendon Press, 1959, pp. 406–18. An excellent analysis of the Peninsular Breton fragments and of the indebtedness of the *Amadís* and other romances.

MARTINS, MÁRIO. "O elemento religioso em Amadis de Gaula." *Brotéria*, 68 (1959), 639–650. Brief but valuable first survey of an important topic.

MENÉNDEZ Y PELAYO, MARCELINO. *Orígenes de la novela*. Madrid, 1905; reprinted in Edición Nacional, 2nd ed., Madrid: Consejo Superior de Investigaciones Científicas, 1961, I, 314–370. The earliest comprehensive critical study, still worthy of serious consultation.

MOTTOLA, ANTHONY. "The Amadís de Gaula in Spain and in France" Ph.D. thesis, Fordham University, 1962. Most recent and very full critical revision, with, however, an unsatisfactory bibliography.

O'CONNOR, J. J. *Amadis de Gaule* [sic] *and its Influence on Elizabethan Literature*. New Brunswick, N.J.: Rutgers University Press, 1970. Good analysis of the fame of the French versions, but naïve and ill informed as regards the Spanish field.

OLMEDO, FÉLIX, S. J. *El Amadís y el Quijote. Soneto famoso de Cervantes al túmulo de Felipe II. El Persiles*. Madrid: Editora Nacional, 1947, pp. 7–14, 17–148. A piece of *belles lettres* rather than scholarship, but the first examination of the *Amadís*'s moralistic content. Rather one-sided.

PLACE, E. B. "The *Amadís* Question." *Speculum*, 25 (1950), 356–66. Ingenious but unconvincing search for a historical basis for the novel. See Jameson's study above.

————. "El *Amadís* de Montalvo, como manual de cortesanía en Francia." *Revista de Filología Española*, 38 (1954), 151–69. Sound piece of research.

————. "Amadís of Gaul, *Wales* or What?" *Hispanic Review*, 23 (1955), 99–107. Successful handling of an important dispute.

————. "Fictional Evolution: The Old French Romances and the Primitive *Amadís* Reworked by Montalvo." *Publications of the Modern Language Association*, 71 (1956), 520–29. Valuable reexamination with some farfetched speculations.

————. "¿Montalvo autor o refundidor del *Amadís* IV y V?" In *Homenaje a Rodríguez-Moñino*, II. Madrid: Castalia, 1966, 77–80. Up-to-date rearguing of an old topic, making use of the 1955 fragments.

RIQUER, MARTÍN DE. *Caballeros andantes españoles*. Madrid: Espasa-Calpe, 1967. Excellent little monograph on the social and cultural background of the age of the *Amadís*.

————. "Cervantes y la caballeresca." In *Suma Cervantina*. Eds. J. B. Avalle-Arce and E. C. Riley. London: Támesis, 1973, pp. 273–92. Another good critical account of the taste for romances during the 1500s and their decline, with full bibliography.

RODRIGUES LAPA, M. *Amadis de Gaula*. Lisbon: Textos Literários, 1941. Portuguese translation reducing the Spanish text to eleven "essential" chapters. See Costa Marques above. M.R.L. adds a rather uncritical essay supporting the Portuguese case, but with some analysis of the novel's originality.

————. *Lições de literatura portuguesa: época medieval*. 7th rev. ed. Coimbra: Coimbra Editora, 1970, pp. 254–65. Mentions fragments but largely repeats the 1941 essay. Restated and slightly enlarged in *Grial*, 30 (1970), 14–28, in which it is claimed that a Portuguese manuscript exists in Madrid.

RUIZ DE CONDE, JUSTINA. *El amor y el matrimonio secreto en los libros de caballerías*. Madrid: Aguilar, 1947. An important study, well documented, of a subject central to the *Amadís* (and other romances).

THOMAS, HENRY. *Spanish and Portuguese Romances of Chivalry: The Revival of the Romance of Chivalry in the Spanish Peninsula, and Its Extension and Influence*. Cambridge: The University Press, 1920. An established classic on the general subject, including a full bibliographical history.

VAGANAY, HUGUES. *Amadis en Français: Essai de Bibliographie.* 1st ed., 1906, in "Extrait de La Bibliofilia"; reprinted New York: Burt Franklin, 1973. A still standard work of reference, covering the period 1544–73, with preliminary material, up to and including the translation of the so-called Book XII, the last of the continuations of the *Amadís.*

WEBER DE KURLAT, FRIDA. "Estructura novelesca del *Amadís de Gaula.*" *Revista de Literaturas Modernas,* 5 (1967), 29–54. The only attempt to analyze the novel's contents in systematic detail. A fundamental contribution.

WILLIAMS, GRACE S. "The Amadís Question." *Revue Hispanique,* 21 (1909), 1–67. Still the best comprehensive survey. Scholarly and judicious.

Mention should be made of a recent doctoral thesis, "El Amadís de Gaula: análisis e interpretación" (Ohio State University, 1974), by Eloy Reinerio González, which, however, at the time of writing, was not yet generally available. Dr. González appears to have covered much of the field of the present monograph, with chapters on the characters, their motivation and beliefs, the narrative techniques including the use of speeches, as well as a review of criticism of the *Amadís* and the *Sergas,* a reexamination of Montalvo's role in reshaping the novel, and a final section on the significances of Urganda.

Index

Abiés, king of Ireland, 28, 49, 81, 82, 113, 128, 151

Abíseos, usurper of kingdom of Sobradisa, 29, 51, 59, 60, 82, 136, 143

Adroid, king of Serolís, 152

Aeneas, 62

Agrajes, cousin and companion of Amadís, 28–31, 34–36, 50, 76, 81, 92, 94, 104, 128, 132

Ajax Telamon, 64

Albadán, evil giant, 82, 101, 154

Alcalá, university, 22

Aldeva, daughter of Adroid, 101

Alexander, the Great, 89

Alfonso X, king of Castile, 45

Alfonso, prince of Portugal, 29, 61

Alhama, 14

Alvarez de Villasandino, Alfonso, 39

Amadís, passim; birth and upbringing, 49, 81; at Lisuarte's court, 49–51; his love for Oriana and its effects, 50–52, 67–69, 72–77, 95–100, 129–30, 136–37, 139–40; his nicknames, 87; on the Ínsola Firme, 128–29, 131–32; in eastern Europe, 53, 64, 65, 117; his combat with the Endriago, 85, 100, 144–45, 163–64; his final battles with Lisuarte, 67, 124, 145; his last adventures, with Darioleta and others, 54, 86, 133–35

Amadís de Gaula, passim; its Arthurian origins, 46–48; authorial comments, 56–72; background, 146–50; use of description, 141–46; geography, 151–55; giants, 163–64; use of humor, 93–95; use of interweaving and other features, 46–56; its language, 155–57;

use of languages, 148–50; use of letters, 72–74; role of love, 95–106, 164–65, magic, 112–35; use of nicknames, 87–88; an outline, 25–37; role of religion, 106–110; use of rhetoric, 43–46; use of secrecy and discovery, 74–78; the *Amadís* "question", 38–42; use of symbols and dreams, 135–40; values and habits of the characters, 88–95

Ambor, son of Angriote and companion of Esplandián, 119

America, 15

Andalod, hermit and friend of Amadís, 84, 87, 109, 110, 139

Andandona, evil giantess, sister of Madarque, 85, 93, 108, 144

Angriote de Estraváus, companion of Amadís, 33, 50, 58, 73, 82, 86, 87, 90, 104

Antebón, father of Brandueta, 101

Antifón, enemy of Celinda, 102

Apolidón, first lord of Ínsola Firme, 29–31, 77, 84, 100, 126–32, 137, 147, 148, 153, 154

Arabia, kingdom of Arábigo, 123, 152

Arábigo, king and ally of Arcaláus, 32, 34, 35, 67, 76, 82, 86, 90, 112, 123, 124, 152, 153

Arbán, king of North Wales, 73, 121, 151

Arcaláus, the evil enchanter, 29, 32, 34–36, 50, 51, 54, 67, 68, 75, 81, 83, 85, 86, 90, 93, 94, 97, 109, 111–13, 118, 121–25, 126, 128, 137, 139, 145, 152, 153

Arco de los Leales Amadores (Loyal